A NEW LOOK AT
LEAN

A NEW LOOK AT
LEAN

Stories, Experiences, and Lessons from the Road

Robert Freck

A NEW LOOK AT LEAN
STORIES, EXPERIENCES, AND
LESSONS FROM THE ROAD

iUniverse books may be ordered through booksellers or by contacting:

iUniverse
1663 Liberty Drive
Bloomington, IN 47403
www.iuniverse.com
844-349-9409

ISBN: 978-1-5320-9982-3 (sc)
ISBN: 978-1-5320-9981-6 (e)

Library of Congress Control Number: 2020917022

Print information available on the last page.

iUniverse rev. date: 10/13/2020

CONTENTS

ACKNOWLEDGEMENTS

This book could not have been written without the help of people who have mentored me, taught me, and provided me guidance along the way. The list is not meant to be complete, but to be illustrative.

John Costanza, who taught me early Lean principles, and had me teach what I didn't know.

Alan Siebenaler, who helped me with my first implementation in Mexico, and taught me how to make a professional presentation.

Linda Miller, who was an implementer, even before I was, and later a colleague on the Lean journey.

Roger Irwin, the Fab Manager, who was rebel enough to let us try lean, and screw up many times.

Stephan Nah of Malaysia, who taught me about kindness, compassion, and the Hash House run.

Rob Jones, who was my "shit shield" to Upper Management, and allowed me to implement Lean, without interference.

Sherry Wilks, who taught me Lean wisdom comes from many places and organizational levels.

Jake Whitehead, who fought many battles for me, even when I didn't know they were being fought.

Norm Bodak, LEI, and other Lean organizations who tried to keep the candle burning for Lean, despite obstacles. And Next Level Partners, who Taught me Strategic Planning.

Andrea Solay, my significant other, who supported me, edited charts, and did everything she could to make this book a success.

CHAPTER ONE
LOOKING AT LEAN IN A NEW LIGHT
*Stories, Experiences and
Lessons from the Road*

Introduction

Most people don't like change and actively resist it. It's human nature at work. And, human nature shows up in the work place, as well. People fear it, dread it, and will do almost anything to prevent it. People fight, flight or freeze to avoid addressing it. Companies, cultures, and countries fear change as well. Progress and evolution are most often made in times of crisis and desperation, but not before. Or, to paraphrase a popular adage, "Better the devil you know than the Angel you don't". I have attempted for the last 30 years to try to convince people, companies and cultures to change. This is my story.

In my younger years, I was an avid long-distance runner. I was a good runner, competitive in my age group, and even the winner of a few races. I would always try for a PR, a personal best, but sometimes, conditions, environment and training would limit the outcome- just like in Lean. And, in golf, during which I managed a single digit handicap for a while, I hit some terrible shots, some pretty good shots and some beautiful shots, where the ball would hit the club perfectly, the shot would soar perfectly through the air, and land on the green, a few yards from the hole, or once or twice, in the hole. It is a golfers' adage that we keep playing the game for those occasional perfect shots. Such is it with Lean. Once one has a really great implementation experience, we crave the next one, like a new PR, like the perfect golf shot and keep trying to have another great race, shot, or Lean experience.

But Lean is difficult, challenging, and perfect shots and PR's are rare. But fulfilling and successful Lean implementations are doable and possible. You just have to know how.

This book is both a personal memoir of my 30 plus year Lean career, as well as an instruction manual about how to have a better Lean implementation experience. My career has been filled with beautiful successes, abject failures, and several places in between, but there have always been lessons. This book will attempt to share these lessons with you and trust you can adapt them to your needs. Most names of companies and individuals' names have been changed out of respect, although from location and industry, it may not be hard for you to identify who they are. And some names have been listed because they were my mentors and teachers, in ways I couldn't possibly understand. I would expect you have made many of the mistakes, as I have, that are listed in this book. Don't feel badly. We are all in the same boat.

Ken Burns is airing this fascinating program on Genes. It speaks of DNA and how it is the key to all life. Not to extend the metaphor too far, but Lean has a DNA, as well. It also has RNA, the messaging piece, and a double helix, of a sort. I will clumsily try to explain this in the subsequent chapters.

What follows is how it sometimes goes badly:

It was late one night in Seattle, and I received a call from a New York number. Quickly doing the time zone math, I realized it must have been 1 a.m. in the Eastern time zone. On the other line was a male voice, apologizing for calling so late, but saying it was very important we talked. He went on to explain that he had just been hired as the VP of Operations for a medical company in New York, and upon starting, he had noticed they had a very large Continuous Improvement effort

2

underway. One of the reasons he was hired was that he had "done Lean" in his previous company, with some success, but really had never got into the details. But in the New York plant, they had been at it for three years, the costs hadn't improved, and to him, it just didn't "smell right". He was wondering if I could spend a week or two in his plant and provide advice.

I had just finished an assignment in Seattle and was free at the time. I asked how the gentleman had heard about me and he said he had attended a conference, where someone I had previously worked for, knew me and said, "he knows what he is doing". For me, that is a very high compliment I hope I have earned. In my 30-year Continuous Improvement career, I have never once done Marketing or Promotion, and was always busy. I have also never consciously "networked"; word of mouth referrals worked for me for a very long time.

The other question I asked about the assignment was how I would be perceived by the current CI organization, and to whom should I share information. I was told they had already spent over $3 million on the project and had yet to see any benefit. He said the current group continuously said he had to be patient, and that the benefits would come, which was my first major red flag.

Benefits from a Lean project should come within three to six months, and if they don't, you are doing something wrong.

So, I came to the plant, and I was introduced to the Lean group, four individuals working on it full time, led by a Manager, who previously was a member of the Consulting Group, who was still actively working in the company. So, eight people working on Lean in a company of 500 people seemed excessive, so I dug into it a bit. The consulting company was a group I had run into before, and frankly, cleaned up their messes many times. They had one mantra "Speed is Life", and everything done was to increase speed. They also were a "recipe" based Lean group, which argued every Lean implementation was the same, and a company just needed to "follow the recipe". Well, Lean is not like cooking Lasagna. My experience in over 30 companies, 50 locations, and eight countries is that every implementation is different. But, more on that, and this story later.

This book is intended to help companies implementing Lean or Continuous Improvement, (which a recent survey says is over 85% of companies). To help them avoid the common missteps and myths, and to provide a common roadmap, not recipe, for a successful Lean journey. Two thirds of implementing companies get little or no gain from their implementation, and to me, this is an avoidable tragedy. And this two thirds are the ones who admit it.

Lean is a powerful methodology to improve a company, but it is a complicated and layered one, it needs to be implemented carefully. Hopefully, my stories of mistakes, failures, moderate successes, and huge improvements can help you, and your company, have a successful experience with Continuous Improvement.

Another company said they had attempted Lean several times, and suggested we name it "Lean 6.0" to suggest a new and better way. Well, this fell by the wayside, as other versions did. But then, what's in a name?

CHAPTER TWO
A BRIEF HISTORY AND HISTORICAL PERSPECTIVE, WELL MAYBE NOT SO BRIEF

Many readers may know or been told of the history of Lean. It has come by many names. History can be useful in guiding thinking and actions going forward. Or, we can keep repeating the mistakes of the past.

The following brief history is with thanks to the Lean Enterprise Institute, who I greatly admire for the basics, which has been mixed in with my memories and experience over the last forty years.

It's not literally true that Lean started with Toyota in post-World War Two Japan, as is commonly believed. It started with Henry Ford in the early 20th century. He started interchangeable parts, moving assembly lines, standard work, and (gasp) "flow production". But Mr. Ford had a problem. He couldn't figure out how to make multiple models on one line, an idea we currently call "Mixed Model Sequencing". It is a concept we continue to struggle with even today. Later in the book there is a company example where 19 different "One Piece Flow" lines were created, all with common processes, instead of figuring out how to mix model sequence. It was a $3 million mistake, with little or no benefit. The good lesson was having interchangeable assembly lines. The bad lesson was not knowing how to do Mixed Model Sequencing.

About 20 years after Mr. Ford, Toyota entered the picture, starting in the 1930's, and intensifying after WW2. There is the famous story, which is part true and part mythology, was when Taiichi Ohno was visiting a US grocery store, and watching loaves of bread sliding down a ramp, and every time one was taken, another one took it's place, the invention of the "Pull System". The good news was the invention of replenishment, the badly learned lesson was about the true meaning of pull, see the Rocks and Water slide.

So, partially from Innovation and partially from necessity, the Toyota Production System (TPS) was invented. Ohno, Kiichiro Toyoda and others were instrumental in this. It was simple and inexpensive, as frankly, they didn't have any money in post WW2 Japan. Not having any money isn't necessarily a bad thing. Today, it is more critical that we understand the philosophy. TPS is very specific to the Japanese culture and the automotive industry. Many companies apply literal TPS to industries where it is an awkward fit. The good lesson was how to do many basic sound manufacturing methods. The bad lesson was not learning that Eastern and Western cultures and Leadership were not the same.

The strategy was, and is always valid, but implementation mechanics sometime go askew.

TPS was largely machine intensive. Right size machines to capacity, make sure the machines were flexible, order them in process sequence, instead of departmental sequence, (huge), and signal the upstream process when more work is needed. Ensure quality at the machine level, rather than with external inspection. Brilliantly simple and very powerful.

The process was summarized in the classic Lean book, which everyone should read or reread, called, "The Machine that Changed the World", by Womack, Jones, and Roos. The Toyota production system was of course that machine. The book was written in 1990, by which time I was deeply into the process we were calling "Just in Time Manufacturing", and later on, "Demand Flow Technology", as espoused by my first mentor, John Constanza.

Principles were described as follows:

- Specify the value desired by the customer
- Identify the value stream for each product providing that value and challenge all of the wasted steps (generally nine out of ten) currently necessary to provide it
- Make the product flow continuously through the remaining value-added steps
- Introduce pull between all steps where continuous flow is possible
- Manage toward perfection so that the number of steps and the amount of time and information needed to serve the customer continually falls

These principles added to Western understanding of Lean, but also led to many misunderstandings and mistakes. For example, it says "identify the value stream of each product", it doesn't say, "create Value Stream maps". It says, "make products flow", not "make one-piece flow". By the way, it never says 'reduce waste", it says challenge it, or have "zero defects", ideas that have cost us numerous years of frustration and cost.

Then, after a while, it birthed TPM and TOC, two essential Lean philosophies implied, but not specifically called out by TPS. These tools were the invention of the Japan Institute of Plant Maintenance, (JIPM) and Eli Goldratt, an Israeli Physicist.

About this time, I was invited on a study mission to Japan. I spent three weeks there studying TPS and actual implementation at a Japanese plant. I was struck by the work ethic, after several 2 a.m. nights, and the tight space the layout of the factories required. But I didn't notice any magic. There was also an interesting approach of relying on the workers to be the process experts, which wasn't originally described in the literature, but was a key element. Also, the concept of "Line Stop", where any worker could stop the entire line, if a quality or process problem was observed. I notice 220 stoppages in one day, most of which were quickly resolved, but written down for later investigation and resolution. Many thanks to Norman Bodak and the Productivity Inc. people for arranging this trip and providing early training and advice to us neophytes.

For this was the late 1980's, and frankly, none of us early converts knew what we were doing. I followed John Costanza's JIT approach and our early success in Mexico was one of the first implementations at both GTE and in Mexico. Doing anything seemed to bring about improvement.

I was also blessed in the late 1980's and early 1990's with other training in Continuous Improvement approaches. The Goldratt Institute taught me TOC, (yes, I am a Jonah); Motorola taught me Six Sigma, although interestingly, they weren't awarding "belts" then, and I learned TPM from a guy named Ed Hartman at a seminar in Phoenix. None of this was called Lean but added to my personal toolbox for improvement methods. I also learned 8D from Ford, because they required it of their suppliers, and I learned other problem-solving methodologies from various sources. I learned Team mechanics from National Semiconductor. Later, I learned A-3 from LEI.

In these "old days", the methods were strictly confined to manufacturing, but we soon began to notice a couple of things. First, the principles seemed applicable to other areas, and secondly, we began to think of interrelated supply chains, where other areas could have a huge impact on Manufacturing. Also, this was in the heyday of MRP systems implementations, which in some regards, conflicted with Pull and Repetitive Manufacturing.

So, we practitioners were working through all of these things, plus pondering how to achieve greater "Employee Involvement", whatever that meant. These were also the days of "Empowerment, Greenfields, Self-Directed Work Forces, and Small Group Activities, and Quality Circles". How to link this with the Lean Work wasn't obvious or even clear. So, we weren't really thinking much about Leadership and Culture, and Lean was pretty much about cost down, and preventing offshore companies from stealing jobs. This was the environment we, and Lean lived in. Semiconductor was particularly vulnerable to Korean and Taiwanese "chip dumping" in the US to gain market share.

So, Lean began to migrate to other company areas and industries. Finance learned about ABC, (Activity Based Costing), although it took years to apply it to Product Costing methodologies.

Product Development learned about DFM and DFA, (Design for Manufacturing and Design for Assembly). "Agile" Manufacturing was also introduced. This was also the era of "Six Sigma", where everyone was training Green Belts, and figuring out how to integrate Six Sigma and Lean. And we mostly lost our way, with all the complexities and integration points, forgetting about principles and core practices. Integration among all these tools into Business system was a long and sometimes painful process. Danaher was a leader in this, but others were slow to follow. Green Belts were primarily doing Lean projects, 5S scorecards and Kaizen events proliferated, and we, again were frankly lost...separated from principles and core objectives. We lost ten years rationalizing Lean and Six Sigma before many companies, including big multinationals, decided the programs were mutually exclusive. We organized many, many SGA's but didn't really empowered them to do anything meaningful. We also didn't really understand the power of problem solving, instead of focusing on "Waste Reduction", and the Seven Deadly Wastes, rather than identifying and solving problems. Another decade lost.

What's in a Name?

In the mid 1980's when I started my journey, the process, new and fresh at the time, was known as JIT (Just in Time) Manufacturing. It then migrated to DFT (Demand Flow Technology), Continuous Improvement, Lean Six Sigma, Operational Excellence, TPS, Repetitive Manufacturing and other names and catchy acronyms. Even tools took on different names; Total Productive Maintenance became Total Productive Manufacturing, 5S became CANDO, and 5 Why became 8D, CEDAC, A-3 and other names. Quick Changeover became SMED, (Single Minute Exchange of Dies, even if there were no dies). Lately, terms such as "Agile" have entered the vernacular.

So, what's in a name? Just adhering to principles and make sense practices, regardless of the name, makes sense to me.

General Principles of Lean

5S vs. VCS

One of the hardest lessons to learn as a Lean person, was not to do 5S. This tool was accepted as a common entry point into lean, it was simple and easy to do, and required no culture or Leadership behavior change. So, thus the trap was set. Implemented on lines, it quickly became a housekeeping program that had little relationship to the original intent and was basically dismissed by employees. 5S scorecards were the laughing stock of lines, but what Lean Leaders relied on as progress. If the artificial 5S scorecard number was higher, we must be making Lean progress. A simple and dangerous hoax. A quick story from experience: I visited Yamaha motorcycle, who were very proud of their "office 5S". A tour revealed all pencils, rubber bands, paper clips and office items labeled and marked. Not quite so much discipline on the floor. Nothing on the line suggested they were identifying and solving problems. But the desks were in good order. But I did learn CANDO from them which made much more sense for me than unintelligible Japanese characters. Clear, Arrange, Neatness, Discipline and Order could, at least be recited in English. The argument here is to replace 5S, with VCS, which stands for Visual Control Systems, which implies the original Spirit of identifying the problems and solutions. The point is to focus on identifying and solving problems, rather than housekeeping. How to make problems visible, is, and always has been the point.

So, let's look at the steps of the Visual control pyramid in detail. But, first, why a pyramid? Because one step builds upon another to resolve problems and reduce defects. And, defect levels narrow, as in a pyramid, as you go up the levels. If you are still a 6 Sigma fan, VCS levels are actually defect levels.

Level 1: Effective communication

Communicate visually, rather than with written instructions. Converting specs to visual One Point Lesson are a good place to start. Be sure, in so many multicultural environments that everyone understands. "A picture is worth a thousand words" is an apt acronym.

Level 2: Labeling

Insure "a place for everything, and everything in its place", is the cliché. Use squares, shadow boards, tape outlines, or anywhere else your creativity takes you. Be sure you have procedures if something is missing.

Level 3: Limiting:

Take the previously labeled areas and limit the amount of material that can go into them. Develop systems that limit getting more if the space is filled. Don't have any room for something that is more than the limit

Level 4: Alarming. Create alarms for problems that occur. These can take the form of line lights and/or audio alarms. The more people complain about the distraction of the alarm, the better. A company I worked for wired the lights to the departmental Engineering computers, which increased the response rate significantly.

Level 5: Prevent Defects from moving on. This implies stopping the process if a defect occurs.

Many are not willing to do this, and it is not effective if Leadership won't stop for a defect. Once the defect is found, ask why and search for countermeasures. Life in the trenches indicates the line may have to be restarted but follow up on the stoppage causes.

Level 6, Fail Safe or Poka-yoke- I have run the "Count the F's" exercise for over 1200 people, and exactly one got it right, and I suspected she cheated" I never got it right, and I was the teacher. Try it if you think I'm wrong. Anyway, the point is, defects are not always noticed, and can "slip through the cracks". Poka-yokes are normally mechanical devices that screen defects before they are passed on. They are difficult and hard to implement. You may only be able to achieve Level 3 or 4, but the journey is worth it.

The Lean question is how high up the pyramid can you go? Most companies can go to at least Level 4, and the thinking process is how can we climb up the VCS pyramid? The fundamental difference is related to Problem Solving instead of Housekeeping. Moving up the pyramid makes Lean progress, whereas a higher 5S scorecard number does not.

Problem Solving:

Problem solving is a rather ubiquitous and generic word. In life, as in work, we all have problems, and we solve them. It is interesting that operators in their daily lives routinely solve problems, but at work are not allowed to, limited by organizational and cultural limitations. What does it actually mean to identify and solve a problem? Are your employees taught this? The essence of Lean.

There are some universals in Lean, regardless of industry or status. One is the idea of problem solving. Let's start with the Philosophy. Problems can be categorized into three categories: Single Cause, Multiple Cause, and Complex Combinational Cause. See charts in Appendix 2:

The problem-solving method used should be based on the type of problem. For single cause, problems, the "just fix it" approach often works, but make sure, as always, you have the problem right, and you get to the root cause. For example, if a fire starts in the plant, the single solution is to get everyone to safety as soon as possible. Later, though, think about what caused the fire and how you can prevent recurrence. Were Leaks contained? Were flammable materials controlled? Where welding sparks contained? Were employees adhering to all safety protocols. Were fire extinguishers all full and up to date? Does the Safety process look at this stuff? Maybe not such a single cause. But, a relatively simple analysis could provide insights. Contain as needed, but don't stop there.

Then, there are multiple cause problems. No one solution allows us to get a handle on it. This generally means a cross functional problem that involves multiple departments and levels. The default problem solving methodology for this is the Fishbone or Ishikawa diagram, which almost everyone is familiar with. The default thinking, culturally, is it not my departments fault. This has been expanded to CEDAC Cause and Effect Diagram with the addition of cards, because it is more Visually compelling, see Appendix 2 below, and other methods. Fords' 8D is a prime example. When incorporated with 5 Why these can be effective problem-solving tools.

A word on 5 Why. Be sure the exercise is well thought out and facilitated. Too often, in my experience, the fifth why is training or Management. Not really what we were looking for here. Make sure you have the problem right before you start.

Also, there is no magic in "five". Causes could be any number, or branch into other areas. Be open to the process.

And then are there preventative countermeasures, not band aids. Human nature suggests people want to do something and move on, then have short memories when the problem returns. Ask, does this permanently fix the problem? If not, what else can we do? Questions for Lean facilitators to ask.

Complex combinational problems are the most challenging, hardest to fix, and most rewarding when you solve one. The basic definition is that if you make one cause better, another gets worse. If you slow down your Production

Line for better quality or more inspections, your ability to meet customer demand can be impacted. If you reduce FGI levels, does your ability to respond to customers decrease?

I found A-3 Problem Solving at a LEI seminar a few years back. It fascinated and intrigued me, and I started to use it with my teams. The most interesting learning point for me, was "Make sure you have the problem right". It doesn't help much to fix the wrong problem. Always ask yourself and your team is the problem is right, without functional and organizational bias. For Example, when we did an A-3 to effectively deploy Supermarkets in an Aerospace firm, the real problem was "Why are we doing Supermarkets? Is there a better way to balance lines and eliminate WIP? Not how do we deploy supermarkets?"

An A-3 is a serious cross functional and cross hierarchy problem solving process that can have major benefits for serious organizations. You can only have a few working at any given time.

Templates of an A-3 Diagram, courtesy of GoLeanSixSigma is in the Appendix section.

CHAPTER THREE
THE BEGINNING, JIT, SEMICONDUCTORS AND TPM

I was a young Engineer working in Illinois, then was offered a chance to transfer to California. As the winter had 30 plus consecutive days of below zero weather, as well as record snowfall, it didn't take me long to decide. Upon arriving in the Bay area, I went to work in a medium size plant, making Transmission equipment. I soon learned they were planning to move to Mexico, due to high building repair costs. I was offered a promotion to go to Juarez, Mexico, and perform a variety of roles. I was to be Materials Manager, IT manager, and basically anything else that needed to be done in a startup, although frankly, I has no experience with any of this. The first thing I tried to do was to get rid of the Asbestos from my office and from the plant.

In any case, we needed a computer system, and decided on an HP 3000 solution. HP sent an Engineer to help us implement, and his name was John Costanza. John later decided to leave HP and start the JIT Institute, and we were his second client. The first client was a firm in Denver, and where I met an implementation specialist named Linda Miller, the Project Leader and his first client. John was our consultant, and I was the Project Manager in Juarez, and I had absolutely no idea what I was doing. John was one of the first people to try to take this idea, previously known primarily in Japan, and to try to adapt it to North American culture. Also, fortunately, for me, I had a General Manager, Alan Siebenaler, who before there was any description of a Lean Leader, clearly was one. He taught me Leadership methods I use to this day. He also taught me how to present to Senior Management, which is key to getting your ideas implemented. But also, not a forum to promise the world, and not being able to deliver. Well, we implemented John's recipe on our PC board line and also our capacitor line and got good results rather quickly. We were quickly identified by Corporate as the first "JIT" (Just in Time) implementation in Mexico. The approach was basically to implement "flow" and quality points in the process, along with Standard work, called Sequence of Events at that time. It was a simple, but highly effective approach. We didn't go for Culture, or Leadership change, just change the Manufacturing process. But, unknowing to us, we had amiable Leadership to drive change.

After four years there, the company decided to open a "Greenfield" factory in Arizona to use all of the latest methods in Manufacturing; Teams, Technology and Equipment and Employee Involvement to get and stay ahead of the competition. I was hired because of my "JIT experience" as the Production Manager, and got to hire a CI Manager, who was, as is today, one of the most brilliant Lean minds I have ever met, who is Linda Miller. I have been blessed to meet many brilliant Lean minds over my career, and to listen to them would be a major benefit. But often they are hidden, buried in the traditional organization. Your job, as CI Leader, is to find them. Linda Miller saved my Lean life. She taught me the process and the pitfalls, and, as an actual Lean leader in a company, taught me the difficulties of implementation. I am forever grateful and honored when she decided to join us in Tempe.

The Greenfield functioned for a while, but after six months, we were bought by a German company, based in Munich, who was the antithesis of Greenfield and new ways. I understand this company has changed since then and have actually embraced Continuous Improvement.

So, they shut us down, and moved us to Albuquerque, and sent a team of "advisors" to monitor our activities. My personal advisor was Herr Strobel, who spent most of his days sitting in my office staring at me. My job was to implement an Interplant System, as we had three plants, and had to get materials between them. I tried to get basic "pull mechanics" into these systems, with some success. Anyway, the "German" experience, didn't suit me, so I decided to join John Costanza as a JIT consultant. What leads us, as Lean leaders to a path we know we are destined for, but until pushed, cannot go to our destiny? Anyway, it worked that way for me.

I went there as his #2 guy as his previous guy, a HP colleague had resigned, during a classroom "rant" about something unintelligible. I was somewhat reluctant to go there, and be portrayed as a "Lean Expert", with exactly one implementation under my belt, but later learned this was the norm for Consultants. So, I taught classes, based on John's "Demand Flow" model, worked on software development to try to develop an interface from MRP Systems to flow, a problem that is still struggling to be solved, and to consult with companies trying to implement JIT. Again, I didn't really know what I was doing. I was sent to an air conditioning plant in Texas, on my first consulting assignment. I noticed the mold presses took a long time to changeover, so I suggested the SMED tool, although it wasn't really part of the recipe. I was then asked to write a book for John, about expanding JIT philosophies to areas outside of manufacturing. Not to sound bitter but the book was published, without as even an acknowledgement as me as a co-author. John Costanza was brilliant JIT/Lean person but had no clue about how to deal with people, and I learned that from him; that without the people side, Continuous Improvement, by whatever name, was doomed to fail. I was also assigned to write a Replenishment

Module, to interface with MRP, and also to co-write a book called "Quantum Leap", not the TV show, to show how JIT could go beyond Manufacturing.

So, we had our inevitable falling out, and I was fired. A client in one of our classes was from an east coast multinational electronics firm and asked me to help them. Upon arriving, I was told of their four divisions, semiconductors, communications, government systems, and copiers. The Semiconductor sector needed the most help. So, I decided to pilot a "JIT" implementation in a Fab in Florida. It was "corporate sponsored", which I didn't understand at the time, but meaning the sector had to try to make it work, or make it fail. Again, meeting a natural Lean Leader, Roger Irwin, before we had an idea of what that meant. We started with Kanban and Flow, and immediately came into a snag. The ION Implanter was not capable of providing sufficient product to upstream and downstream processes. This was an important lesson to learn; equipment must be capable enough to support Lean. This led me to TPM, first in a seminar, then to training and certification from JIPM, the Japan Institute of Plant Maintenance, a subsequent study mission to Japan with Ford. Yes, I am a certified JIPM instructor, but would also caution to be leery about credentials and certifications. Nothing can take the place of your instincts and knowing what to do on the floor.

TPM also led me to Eli Goldratt' s TOC, Theory of Constraints, which argued to identify the constraining part of the process and give it sufficient resources to break the constraint. In the Fab pilot, it was clear the Ion Implanter was the constraint, and we had to fix the issues to assure smooth flow. Well, the first assumption is always the equipment is always down too much, and the second point is the Maintenance argument that it is not downtime, and they have the data to prove it. The first step is to determine the OEE Overall Equipment Effectiveness, which has been the cause of one the biggest Lean mistakes over the years. OEE is not Availability times Performance Efficiency x Rate of Quality, it is in fact Actual Production divided by Theoretical production, and then the task is to bin the losses. This is the topic of a future chapter and be left here for now.

We focused on the Ion Implanter, ensuring the supply to Photolithography and eliminating the Constraint. Practically, this meant increasing the Kanban size in front of the implanter and insuring adequate supply to Photo. This simple solution made the system work, and FAB metrics all improved.

This Florida Semiconductor firm wanted to fire this guy, me, except for the fact that it was a "Corporate Initiative", that maybe, just maybe, was in their best interest to be proved wrong. But, maybe, the thought was the guy may have something here. The Top leadership invited me to introduce this concept to their Semiconductor operations, worldwide. This included six fabrication facilities in the US, and six in Southeast Asia. Two of the sites were recent acquisitions of other US Midwest Semiconductor firms.

These acquisitions weren't Intel or TI, but rather Semiconductor smaller players in the industries. I was tasked with doing the Continuous Improvement work in these sites, as well.

The difference was, these were union sites, in the Midwest, and imbedded in their cultures. Upon arriving at the Ohio site, I was with the VP and he went and a rant about the Sparky dog, the symbol of the required company in the lobby, that this was the new company's culture now.

There is a story on this later. But what was this Culture? It was basically drive hard for stretch targets. There was no clear definition of what that was. Upon visiting the Pennsylvania site, I was told the constraint was the piece of equipment that diced the Silicon into wafer sizes. Upon investigating, I learned that the equipment stopped every 20 minutes or so, due to an "Auto Alarm" that would go off, if no attention was paid. An operator could simply push a reset button, but was not allowed to, due to union restrictions. Asking why operators could not press the reset button, it turned out to be a matter of power and trust. We managed to change this in the next union negotiation, and the constraint was removed, and Fab flowed better. Simple solutions to simple problems.

When I first stated in the Semiconductor industry, I didn't know a computer chip from a potato chip. But, quickly, I came to realize a few things. One is that cleanliness is everything. I observed Class 100 to Class 10 to Class 1 Cleanrooms. Gowns, suites, masks and air showers were the order of the day. Classes of Clean rooms are referred to denote the number of particles of size 0.5 μm or larger permitted per cubic foot of air. All are cleaner than a hospital operating room. Yet, in areas not directly exposed to the wafer, dirt, dust and particles were readily apparent, and with air flow, could easily seep into the Fab wafer operation. We tagged 212 areas in one set of equipment in a Wafer Fab once. So, the 5S approach seemed a logical place to start. But the Japanese characters and translations always seemed foreign to me, as did the later versions of 6S, which included safety. So, I changed the acronym to CANDO, learned from Yamaha, and later to VCS and then Initial Clean and Inspection from the TPM process. More on the rationale of this later.

The main Learning point was that, if the Equipment wasn't flexible and reliable, Pull and Lean had no chance.

Then, it was on to Southeast Asia, to the Singapore and Malaysia sites, which did Assembly and Packaging for the Wafers produced in the US. These were high labor-intensive operations which is why they were there, and machines were basically, Die attachers, Wire Bonders and Test Equipment, and lots of them. We started with 5S, another huge Lean mistake, remembering we are already in Clean room environments. A funny story is, in a Malaysian plant, I pointed out to the Plant Manager the need for 5S. He said they were doing it, just go check out the restrooms. Going into the restroom, I noticed a sign above the men's urinal giving an instruction about how to stand over the toilet. I laughed and asked the Plant Manager about it later. He said the majority of the male workers came from the rice paddies and fields, and normally squatted over a hole in the ground to "do their business". Lesson learned about different methods in different cultures. Lean must be adapted to the culture in place. I changed it to Initial Clean on equipment, and things went better.

Training of the Operators was big in those days. I never was sure how much of it was absorbed, even with translators. But what was always stressed, but never strongly enough was problem solving, at the floor level, and their role in identifying and solving problems. That was a lesson, and it could have been pushed more strongly But, the culture was patriarchal and hierarchical, and one takes what one can get. This went along with the misused term in TPM, of "Autonomous Maintenance", which was never meant for the operators to maintain the equipment on their own, but rather to "take care" of the equipment as their own.

My first client was a multinational Florida Semiconductor firm. After two and half years there, the original Fab Manager, a corporate Quality guy and myself thought this was great stuff, and we should join up to spread these ideas word wide. Thus, birthed IMC, the company I founded and worked, worldwide for twelve years. The other two individuals had long and successful careers with the Florida company, but never joined me.

So, I worked very hard in the Semiconductor industry for this time, primarily on the Equipment side, getting OEE's up, avoiding capital expenditures during up cycles, driving cost down during down cycles, and always raising awareness about equipment problems and issues. It's interesting that I got basically my start, in High Tech, as I really took many things for granted, e.g. Quality Systems, Cleanliness, Operating Standards. And most importantly, "Moore's Law", which said every 18 months, chips must get twice as small, twice as powerful, and at half the cost as the previous period. This created a fast-paced environment, that kept everyone on their toes. For me, that was soon to change, as I embarked on my next experience. But first, some Fab stories.

Fab Stories

I have implemented Lean in 14 Fabs, in eight companies in my career. They are all unique but have some commonalities. They always include TPM/TOC, VCS. and Pull. The stories below are sometimes educational and illustrative, and sometimes just stories. As a wise Spiritual advisor once taught me, "Who would you be without your story?". Below are my stories.

Fab 59 Florida

This was my first exposure to a Wafer fab, and my first major solo consulting project. And, I clearly had no idea what I was doing. Thankfully, I had a great partner in the Fab manager, who was somewhat of a rebel in the operation. He also had the first "open Fab" around in those days, which means there were no "bays", and everything was in one line of sight. So, we started with "Pull"". Here, this meant a series of 108 laminated clean room Kanban cards, indicating when the next process needed work of a specific level. In Photolithography, since we had Coat/Align/Develop modules, we used Kanban Squares and a board to control flow throughput. See the Attachment section for examples. And, boy, did I learn what Pull is all about. It's not about sending signals to the upstream process for more work, as much as it is identifying where problems and disconnects in the process are. Most of you are probably familiar with the famous "rocks and water" slide, which says, "Lower the inventory, uncover the problem". So, in the Fab 59 Lean world, with the inventory lowered, the problems appeared. And the first one was the Ion Implanter, which fed Photolithography. The implanter was not thought of as a problem before, because it had "good uptime". However, changeovers, an abundance of Test wafers, and unbalanced flow were killing the input to Photo. So, we had found Herbie.

After pull was implemented, nothing got better in the Fab. Senior Leadership started to wonder what we were doing, saying, "Lean doesn't apply to our industry" was a common refrain at the time. Anybody heard that one before? So, out of desperation, I read JIPM's book on TPM, and went to a seminar in Phoenix, by a guy named Ed Hartman, on the same TPM. And, lightbulbs came on. Again, I was young and inexperienced, too inexperienced to know what seemed to be obvious. So, we started TPM on the Implanters, working on the "losses", although we didn't really have a language or a process for this. And, we added Kanban cards to the process, to never starve the constraint. On the plane ride home, I wrote a paper on "temporary" Kanban cards, to give the Plant

Manager up to four cards to deploy in the event of changes in mix, quality issues and the like. The reluctance to allow people to deploy these cards is obvious, but in this case, they were used discreetly.

Very quickly, the constraint went away, the Fab flow was restored, and we moved forward.

There were of course, other issues in flow, and in constraints, but the team solved them quickly. Remember, that Kanbans are designed to resolve problems, first and primarily.

The team was quirky, eccentric, and brilliant. Kind of like how Fab people are.

Our team meeting was primarily held on Wednesday's and Friday's, at a local restaurant called "Friendly's". We chose those meeting days in order to try to beat the promotion that, if the food wasn't delivered in ten minutes or less, it was free. Wednesday was Senior day, and Friday was the busiest day, so that was the driving factor, so we met twice a week to get free food. We were successful in obtaining free food about 30% of the time, until eventually they ended the promotion, but we continued the "Friendly Lean meetings" for quite some time. If your company is looking for a great Team building exercise, consider Friendly's as an alternative to Paint Ball, falling into each other's arms, or other activities. Or, adopt Star points, as described in a later section, or other methods, to hold effective Team meetings.

Another lesson was just about anything can be accomplished with a great team. I was an inexperienced consultant, and I think that was an advantage, and couldn't take on the snooty, "I know everything air", as is sometimes seen. I also didn't have a text book, so couldn't use one to implement, instead relying on my teams' wisdom and common sense. These are lessons that lasted a lifetime

We also alarmed each process with Line lights and/or alarms, so that quick response was required to every line stoppage. Maintenance and Engineering hated this system, but line time response to problems fell dramatically. Sometimes, walking through the Fab, the alarms would be noisy and alarming, which was the point. "Turn that xxx, ing alarm off", became a common Fab refrain. So, pull TPM/TOC and pull were lessons I learned and continued to implement. The processes and problem-solving tools continued to evolve.

Fab 2 in San Antonio Texas

This is more story than educational, as the typical TPM Equipment Improvement process was employed and implemented. The story is the internal battle between Apple and Android products. The parent Japanese company had decided that everybody worldwide would migrate to Android, and the site were big Apple users. Coming in on my first Friday, everyone in the plant was wearing "Apple" black T shirts, all office employees, and many Fab employees underneath their clean room suits. I don't know if anything came of the protest, but TPM continued. Regardless of platform, we continued with the TPM and EI process and made sustainable gains.

Fab in Scotland

I was deployed by a multinational to Dundalk, Scotland. This again, is mostly story, as the typical TPM was deployed and effective. So, first of all, the weather in Scotland is known for its foggy and inclement weather. One day, during TPM training, during a break, there was a mass exodus from the class. Everyone headed for the beaches, and as rarely happened, the sun came out, a rare event in this part of the world. I joined them, and the picture of the pale skinned excited engineers was inspiring and inspirational.

I also asked to go to a Soccer match between Celtic and Rangers, just to have the experience. I was advised by the Fab people not to attend, as they would be concerned for my safety. So, instead, they took me "pub hopping", which included starting with English pints, and then switched to bars for Vodka. I carefully limited my intake, as I had training the next day, but my students did not. They partied until after two A.M. and went home.

The next morning, everyone rolled in for training and Fab assessments. All the previous nights party people looked fresh and ready for work, which kind of amazed me.

A final story about driving in Scotland. I was somewhat used to driving in Europe on the opposite side of the road, roundabouts, and the like. But I forgot about stop signs being on the road surface, rather than on a sign. So, this causes a rather nasty accident for me, heading home, after a two week visit to the plant. The crash was totally my fault, as I ran the stop sign, I didn't see the marking on the road and it, caused significant damage to a Mercedes, which had "just gotten out of the shop", after a two month stay. The plant took care of the problem and got me to my flight on time. The key was the bonding with the team, and the benefits that came from that. Not to be the "Corporate Consultant", but in fact, a member of the team.

Others

There are many other Fabs, and many other stories, some of which are listed below.

AMI and 9/11

In Idaho, I was called in, as one of the Fabs was unhappy with their consultants, the Timebased Management guys. The TPM/TOC and EI processes, described below, made much more sense to them than the "Speed is Life" people who believed everything should be sacrificed for reduced cycle time. Then, one day, some terrorists plowed some planes into New York City Twin towers, and much of life in America changed. Being in a Mountain time zone, we got the news a bit later than others, and it didn't really change the Lean implantation, but it affected everyone's life.

There did seem to be a new determination and seriousness after the events of 9/11, especially in our military applications. But, life, as it tends to do, went on. We made medical devices, one of which included pacemakers for government officials, and somehow work took on new intensity, as if this industry needed it.

We saved over a million dollars in Fab costs, another half million in Product Costing adjustments, and an estimated $2 million in Fab capacity increases that allowed incremental business.

After two years, I was called into the Global VP's office, and after being told I had done a great job in my two plus years there, my contract wasn't being renewed because, "I didn't think like they did". My reply was that I thought that was the point, but I was asked to move on anyway.

Robert Freck

Assembly and Test Stories

TPM in the Backend processes of Semiconductor

Assembly and Test in the Far East presented new challenges than in the States Wafer Fabs. The primary one was language. Simultaneous translators are often required. Also, it is more difficult to drive Employee involvement and participation in largely partisan and patriarchal cultures. But experiences in Singapore, Malaysia, Indonesia, and Thailand taught me the "wisdom of the process", and the wisdom of the operator who worked in it.

Fabrication was generally done in the states, and assembly and test processes done in Asia, which had higher labor content and was considered less complex. My experience includes eight Assembly and Test facilities for four companies. Here are some stories.

5S in Melaka:

I was trying to drive 5S, back when I believed in it, in a plant in Melaka, Malaysia. The plant manager was a friend and advocate of mine. During a meeting, I took a rest room break, and noticed a sign over the men's urinal, a "One Point Lesson", on how to go to the bathroom. I though this a bit extreme and overboard, and upon returning to the Plant Managers' office, mentioned it to him. His comment was "Robert, you don't understand, many of my employees come from rural areas, and have never seen a public urinal before. They usually "do their business in Public holes in the ground". Lesson learned.

Singapore 4 C's

This was the most prosperous city state in SE Asia at the time. It had a reputation of being a "fine city", not only because of its fine culture and public transportation system, but because it would fine citizens for just about everything, spitting, jaywalking, you name it. A friend, the local Lean coordinator, in his early 30's, talked about dating in Singapore. According to him, one needed 4C's to be able to get a girl to date you- a Cell phone, a Car, a Condo, and a Condom. I don't know if this was true, but that was his belief. Equipment Costs were higher there, and they had to work the process to ensure they could keep the work they had.

Kuala Lumpur, Malaysia

This was a large site, with 4000 employees, and several lines. They were highly successful with TPM and won the Prime Ministers award for excellence. The Ford Pull fiasco is listed below. They did excellent TPM work, largely following the TPM process described below. But the stories are actually more interesting. The Lean leader, Stephan became one of my best friends. The plant was allegedly "haunted" and at times when I was there the plant was evacuated to clear the ghosts/ spirits from the plant. There was actually a man contracted by the plant, who was called in to remove the Spirits, called a Boamah, loosely translated as "Witch Doctor". He would come in, do his thing, and the operators would return to work. He would come into the plant, chant, talk to the spirits, and convince them to leave. This was not explainable to my US colleagues, but actually helped the process. The machines were "blessed" by the Boamah, did this give them higher OEE's?

We had a weekly Saturday activity during my stays, called "Hash House runs". This came from Australia, and was adapted to the Malaysian culture, which meant we ran through the jungle. Someone came out and laid a "paper trail" which were to be followed by the runners. "False trails" were laid, which were intended to have the lead runners lose their way, thus equalizing faster and slower runners. So, one time, I was running in the Hash, and fell into a sinkhole. I felt a snap in my ankle and incredible pain. My friend Stephan came up, and carried me to the start, where I said I needed to go to the emergency room. He gently suggested, "Let's do something else instead". I was in too much pain to argue, so we drove through muddy roads to a small village way off in the wilderness. There were a series of huts, with no electricity, plumbing, or running water. I was taken into one of the huts, where a 90-year-old blind man, minimally dressed, who addressed Stephan in Bahasa Malay, Stephan described my situation. I was directed to lay on a table, where the old, blind man chanted, messaged, and rubbed Tiger Balm lotion on my ankle. It was excruciating painful. Stephan drove me back to my hotel, and I went to sleep. I woke up with no pain, no swelling in the ankle, and actually went for a run the following morning. I later learned this was the same Boamah, Witch Doctor, who was employed in the plant to remove evil spirits. How often are "false trails" laid for you for Lean solutions? How often are "Witch Doctors", disguised as consultants, brought in to help implement Lean. Thinking points.

As a side note, the Hash house runs concluded with heavy beer drinking and a big dinner. But, in the Malaysian version, one could acquire things in the jungle. Such as leeches. The leaches would be burned off people's appendages and placed in the beer. This would make the beer red in color and somewhat less appetizing, but the Malaysian version of the Hash was fun and unusual. See the Kanban section for the Ford Motor Company Pull story at this site.

Indonesia

The plant in Indonesia was trained and guided in the Equipment Improvement process and executed it well. At the time the country was in a bit of turmoil, as the country's long-standing dictator was in the process of being overthrown. I went for an early morning run and saw tanks with soldiers rolling through the streets. It was considered removing expatriates from the country, but it was decided to keep operations going.

I also met the first person I had known with multiple wives. He had four wives, and the plant joke was he needed one more for five wives, a takeoff of 5 Why's. He was the local plant manager and a good guy. Over dinners and discussions, he described to me how it worked in their culture. Although one wife was enough for me, and sometimes one too many, I got a different perspective on the culture and beliefs.

Philippines

I had clients in the Manila area and Cebu. The poverty was overwhelming to me at times. The people in the plant in Cavite were willing and provided less resistance than stateside. Anyone from the US was considered somewhat of a guru, although my objective was just to fit in. Operators were trained and were comfortable enough to express frustrations about Management obtuseness, not listening to problems, and being dismissive. I recognized this as a national cultural issue, as well as a company issue. But, still one that needed to be resolved. So, the company needed to be more participative and listen to operators, but culturally, didn't really know how. Working with Management on these issues was difficult, but ultimately beneficial. The experience and intelligence of the operators also really struck me. Often, with no more than sixth grade educations, they knew more about the process they worked in than many of the Engineers. Management was reluctant, in this culture, to accept this, but generally, and slowly came around. I was always struck by the opulence of the Shangri-La hotel, and then going for my morning runs, the abject poverty of the surrounding area. Meet the company where it's at and move them forward from there.

Thailand

I was employed in a Plant in rural Thailand, 90 minutes from Bangkok and in a lovely rural setting. I trained over 300 people with the aid of simultaneous translators, and the process progressed. But, the most interesting parts remain the stories. First of all, the Plant Manager, and an expat, was an old school guy, and I was given an instruction to evaluate him, which I hated to do but was part of the job. He didn't want change, and that was not what we were looking for in Lean Leaders. His boss, the VP, insisted I come in and implement at least TPM, and I did so, and evaluated the person as a leader who would and could not drive and sustain a Lean culture. I, as a contractor, should not have been allowed that authority, but, in truth and in fact, someone needed to do it.

Culture at the plant was interesting. There were about a dozen "expats", and they formed a close group, both in and out of work. They basically ran the plant. Once a month, they would go to Bangkok for some "R and R". I should have suspected what that meant, but at the time, was very naïve.

Once time, I accompanied them. I was told we were going to dinner in an area called "Pot Pong". Which was the Red-Light district of Bangkok, legal but shady. We walked in a bar, and were noticed dozens of naked, or close to naked women. Some of them approached our group and encouraged us to buy them drinks. I got to talking to one, who spoke some English. Not to be sexist or prejudiced, but Thai woman are among the most beautiful in the world. Her story was that she came from the north of Thailand, lived on a farm with her family. They had a bad harvest, and she had to come to Bangkok, and sell her body, so her family could eat. I pulled a $20 bill out of my pocket, handed it to her, with no strings attached, and looked for my colleagues, who had disappeared. I never found them until the following Monday, and of course incurred a lot of good-natured ribbing about the girl.

I later heard about a Senior VP, who every time he came, "went crazy with the woman". So, it's not surprising that the term "ugly American" became quite popular in the region. On the production lines, the operators were diligent and hard working and willing to learn. They kept their equipment clean and identified problems, which was the Lean objective.

The TPM and Equipment Improvement process was implemented in all of these operations. Changes in flow, culture, and Leadership were harder. The operators were enthusiastic about TPM and Autonomous Maintenance and progress was made.'

CHAPTER FOUR
TPM AND THE EQUIPMENT IMPROVEMENT PROCESS, AND OTHER "PILLARS" AS WELL

Leaderships Role in the Process

Forget "Leadership Standard Work". It was a consulting Fad for a while but has never yielded any value in my experience. I did do a Leadership exercise once, however that I did find valuable. On the left side of a piece of paper, we listed the top ten things we did with our time, sequenced in most time to least time order. The right hand side, listed in the same way, the things we found most important to us. Then, Step 3 is to compare this lists. Almost always, there are significant disconnects. Look at how to align the lists more closely. For example, instead of having a "morning meeting" with staff for an hour, spend 15 minutes on that, then go to the floor for Gemba's and Huddles.

There is a real difference in leadership "supporting the process", and doing the things required to make it work. The JIPM handbook says TPM is a "company sponsored activity". Translation, mandatory, rather than voluntary. But, difference in Japanese and American cultures persist. Leadership needs to provide the resources required to make the process work. For the EI team, this is 4-6 hours a week for 9 months, and for the SGA's 2-4 hours a week for the same duration. This is nonnegotiable and with no exceptions. This is not only core team members, but also support groups, such as IT that can provide assistance. Leadership needs to clearly communicate the urgency of the need for this process, stating to all the strategic and tactical need for the initiative. No "program of the month" mentality here. Leadership needs to attend reviews and ask what they can do to clear "Red" items, e.g. Action plan items that are late. Finally, leadership needs to celebrate success, a gathering, an award ceremony, something,

And, it needs to be sincere, not a rote thing that's supposed to be done. This is not natural for many leaders. There can't be too many of these "strategic objectives", limit it. Two or three at the most. Trust the facilitator. Outside eyes is a key advantage, but the person needs to know what they are doing. No resources, no progress, is the mantra. It's not part of the regular work, until it is, meaning that enough other activities can be eliminated or transferred to make available time.

Leadership Development

A word or two about Leadership development. The owners agreed to do the NLP (Next Level Partners) Lean Leadership training, which was composed of 12 one-hour lessons. What is Leadership training? This should be mandatory for any Lean implementation.

Here's a common definition:

The Lean Management System is comprised of elements including process metrics, leader standard work, A3 problem solving, accountability boards, suggestion systems and Gemba walks.

Some of these elements make sense, some not so much. This book is not meant to be an exhaustive list of Leadership trainings and behaviors, but just sharing experiences.

Lesson 1: Do the time/priority list described above. See how you can modify actions to make the list align better. If Lean is important, spend time on it, and not just in reviews.

Lesson 2: is on Gemba walks and Huddles:

Leadership needs to be trained on how to do Gemba walks and Huddles. Many Leaders walk around the plant, greet employees, ask how it's going, and return to their offices. This is not a Gemba walk or a huddle. It may be helpful to script a Gemba walk, and at first, as the Lean leader, accompany the Leader on a walk. They need to pay attention to the following: What are the problems have been identified and what is the response to these problems. Is there an easy visual way to identify problems and responses? Are there any abnormalities you can notice?

Are inventory levels where they should be? Are defect and other metrics clearly noted? Write these things down and share them with your staff members. Huddles are 5-10-minute meetings on a line with a small group. These are not social gatherings. This is tough for Leadership to grasp this. Ask if problems are clearly visible, are they being addressed, and how can you, the leader help? Scribe the issues and share with staff. What is being escalated to you, that for some reason, must be escalated to you. These are normally cross functional issues.

Lesson 3 is on Process metrics: Leadership asks the question; Are we measuring the right things? OEE is an example of a Lean measurement, rather than downtime. Are the measurements correct, fair and not "gamed"? Do we have countermeasures in place where KPI goals are not being met? Do we even have the right problems identified, down to the root cause level? This is in part the power of A3, the prime Leadership problem solving tool to employ. Most people know A-3 as a paper size.

It is used in Problem Solving as it is concise, fits on one page, and has all the elements of root cause analysis and preventative analysis. The first step is to state the problem, and always ask, "Do we have the problem right?". And often we don't. For example, the Problem is stated as "Manufacturing costs are too high?". Is it true? In many cases, the problem is the Product Costing system, the Sales commission system, the innovation systems, or something else? But it is easy and common to blame Manufacturing costs for everything. As Leadership, it is important to study the root cause of the problem, and the second order effect, as described in the CEDAC diagram above.

Lesson 4 is on Decision Making: Ask, what decisions can I have made at a "lower level" of the organization. There are matrixes to help you decide this, but intuition works pretty well. If you have trouble coming up with anything, you have the wrong list, or they have the wrong leader.

A commentary on Culture:

First of all, culture is hard to change, yet Lean insists on changing company culture, as well as Leadership changes and deploying tools, but what does that really mean? What is company culture, can it be changed, and if so, how. And how does it inform and influence Lean implementation.

Before reading the expert version below, let's look at it simply, and maybe you can skip to the next chapter:

1. Make sure Leadership "gets it". How can I serve versus "what's in it for me"? Rarely seen and impossible to fake.

2. Make problems good, rather than something to be covered up.
3. Track the right things, know what to do when it's not going well.
4. Create a "no blame" environment.
5. Foster interdepartmental and cross functional activity.
6. Push decision making down. This is hard for many.
7. Equalize Pokes and Strokes.

The question becomes, can Lean work without Culture and Leadership change. The answer is somewhat. It can be a good golf shot that winds up in the sand trap.

Wafer Processing and Equipment

Producing a wafer is a detailed, difficult, time consuming process. We won't go into the details here, but in the words of an industry expert, "it's all about the equipment, stupid". A typical fab would have 80 or 90 pieces of critical equipment, each costing millions of dollars.

Photolithography, the heart of the process, would be $8 to $12 million a "cell", consisting of a coater, a photolithography machine, and a developer, plus associated Inspection equipment, and a typical Fab would have three of four sets. A typical Fab would have $100-$200 million in equipment. It was essential to keep this equipment in top shape, not only keep it up and running, but also with prime performance efficiency and quality. Unfortunately, during this time, there wasn't really a viable system for addressing this. "Uptime" was still the primary equipment measure, and as long as a tool was "up", it was okay. Along with Eli Goldratt, an Israeli physicist, who wrote "The Goal", and developed TOC,

(Theory of Constraints) and JIPM, the Japan Institute of Plant Maintenance, which invented TPM (Total Productive Maintenance), I developed the Equipment Improvement Process (EIP), which I used and taught during my years in Semiconductor, and beyond. We will detail the steps below. Note the Herbie reference below:

1. Change the Performance Metric (KPI) from Uptime to OEE.
2. Find Herbie. In the book, "The Goal", Herbie was the overweight Boy Scout who couldn't keep up with the troop, preventing them from reaching camp before dark. So, the troop came up with the "Drum, Buffer, Rope" approach to get them to the camp on time. The troop leader was also a Plant Manager, and adopted the approach to his plant, with great success. He identified the constraint by the simple approach of seeing where the inventory was. Today, we look at the differential between required OEE and actual OEE, which we will discuss in a little while.
3. Form and Equipment Improvement Team (EIT). Have eight cross functional members from Operations, Maintenance and Engineering. Have these be the best people in the organization. Form an SGA, (Small Group Activity) composed of line workers to support the EI team. Charter them from top Leadership. A trained facilitator should lead the first cycle, and perhaps the second. Create "Starpoint's" for Leadership of key project elements. See chart below.
4. Determine the OEE tracking mechanism. Contrary to popular myth and belief, OEE is not Availability x Performance Efficiency x Rate of Quality. It is simply Actual Production divided by Theoretical

Production, where theoretical production is hours operated x theoretical rate per hour, TRH. TRH can be dicey to establish, one may use the Equipment Manufacturers spec, the best the tool has ever done, or the "wisdom of the group". Don't be shocked if the number for OEE is low, 42% is about average, in my experience. Have the team develop a method to track this on a daily basis. An automated method is best, a PLC of some sort, but an Excel Spreadsheet will do. FYI, the original formula from Japan is unworkable because Performance Efficiency is extremely difficult to define, plus it doesn't get us any closer to the Equipment Losses than the direct method.

5. "Bin" the Equipment Losses. Categorize or bin them into 6-9 categories, which will slightly vary by toolset, but will likely look very similar to the list below. Note where you cannot define a bin and find a way to define it. Bin these losses to hours per week equivalents.

   a. Unplanned Downtime- losses of more than five minutes, requiring Maintenance intervention

   b. Planned Downtime- Actual PM time on the machine. Amortize monthly, quarterly, and annual maintenance into a weekly average.

   c. Set up time. Time from last product out of one model to first model in to the machine of the next model. That is, the machine can be down for an hour, but the setup time is only 20 minutes. Test wafers/quals, first piece inspections could be the difference.

   d. Minor Stoppages- Less than five minutes of downtime, and able to be fixed by the operator. In a Pennsylvania Fab, the first step of the process was to take silicon and convert it into raw wafers. There was only one machine, and it was identified as a constraint, as it wasn't keeping up with elevated production demand. Leadership was considering a second machine, or subcontracting work to an outside firm. I was asked to look into the situation. The first thing I noticed was that the machine alarmed and stopped frequently. About five times a shift. When it alarmed, the operator had to call maintenance, as she was not permitted to hit the Reset button on the tool, due "to the Union contract". Maintenance would take about 15-20 minutes to show up, and, upon arriving, simply hit reset, and leave. This was a loss of about three hours a day, as the loss was larger on the off shift. In TPM terms, this was a 15% loss. This was a Minor Stoppage but became Unplanned Downtime. The first intervention was to allow the operator to hit the reset button. This saved half the loss. The second step was to analyze why the reset button was going off in the first place. It was simply an Equipment Supplier specification that needed to be reset. The gain of 20 hours a week of production broke the constraint and allowed Production to flow better. Leadership was, somehow surprised by this analysis, and asked for more cases where operators could step up for minor issues. This became a prime discussion for the next union contract negotiation.

e. Idle Time. There are two types of Idle Time. No work and no operator. If chosen as a theme, subdivide into these two categories.

     f.   Slow Speed. The Difference between the amount produced during running time, and the theoretical amount producible during running time. This is likely an elusive number, perhaps better left to a later cycle.

     g.   Rework time. All time spent reworking or retesting questionable product. Either on the equipment, or off it.

     h.   Scrap time. All time spent producing product that turned out, now or later, to be bad.

     i.   Startup Loss- The time it takes to restart a machine, after it has not been running. Tracked to first product out.

6.   Chose improvement theme

     a.   Pick one or two bins of the above losses to improve over the next 13 weeks. Why 13 weeks? I was taught by my Japanese mentors that 13 weeks is enough time to get to root cause and implement countermeasures, but not too long for the team to dawdle or overanalyze. It has proved to be effective for me.

7.   Use Lean problem-solving tools to analyze the losses. Do this as a team. I always liked to use the CEDAC tool, (Cause and Effect with the Addition of Cards), (Attachment 1) as it is simple visual and participatory. A-3 is also a good problem-solving tool.

8.   Track the Loss bin weekly. Create a chart. Monitor the OEE as well, but worry about the loss bin performance, not the OEE. Loss bins can shift from one to another quickly.

9.   Develop an action plan. Prioritize the Action plan, using the Impact Control Matrix. Chart below. We call this a W3I, who, what, where, when impact.

10. Meet weekly to review loss performance and Action plan. Red, Yellow, Green Action plan items. Discuss Reds and take additional countermeasures. Also, review and synergize SGA work, (Appendix 2).

11. Facilitate teamwork between Maintenance and Operations. Break the paradigm of "You run, I fix", into "we are mutually responsible for keeping the equipment in Optimal condition". This takes time, and what we call "Culture change" This is the first step forward for an operation. A memorable story, when I was working with a second shift team in an Idaho fab, I walked into a breakroom, with most of the Maintenance staff sitting there and playing cards. I asked if there was something they be doing for the Equipment or for the Team. I will never forget the response. Robert, they said, laughing, "You have to understand, if there is nothing for us to do, that's a GOOD THING." Was it really? Could there be something to be done with training operators on Autonomous Maintenance or Equipment improvement items. More on this later. Start discussions of "The Transfer Zone". This is a discussion of maintenance tasks that could be done by operators. They are binned into "Red, Yellow", and Green", with Red being always to be done by Maintenance, Yellow tasks could be done with training, and green tasks could be done by operators immediately. Start discussion between Production and Maintenance on these tasks, and the value it could bring to the organization.

While all of this is going on, the SGA is conducting, "Initial Cleaning and Inspection", which is somewhat of a misnomer, as it is more of an inspection than a cleaning. They are given Red dots and instructed to place the dot on any equipment abnormality, with a number on it. They write the number on the dot, and scribe it onto a Post It or notebook. This is a twohour initial process, during which many abnormalities are identified. This is done with all Production Operators and key others. The record in my experience is 212, on an Ion Implanter. This list is then analyzed by who can fix the problem, one code for an operator fix, one for a Maintenance fix, one for a Facilities or Engineering Fix. This log is kept as part of the EI Teams records and reviewed once a month for progress. It's interesting what the impact of the dot is. The Fab Director was walking through one day, and asked the Production Manager, "What the xxxx are all of these dots for". Having had it explained it to him, the Fab Director was surprised at all had been found, and quickly thereafter, many of the dots were cleaned up. Focus on dots you can't fix and find out why.

After 13 weeks, the team, almost always has success, which should be celebrated, both by the team and the organization. Have a debrief meeting, discussing positives, negatives, and lessons learned. Then, move on to the next cycle, and repeat Steps 4-10.

Communication

As with all Continuous Improvement activities, visual communication, at the point of the work, is key. The "Activity Board" is a good way to do this in TPM. (See Appendix 4). A specific four panel layout is suggested.

The Down cycle

Semiconductor has always been known for "Boom or Bust" cycles, periods of high demand, followed by periods of very low demand. So, TPM approaches needed to change with the demand cycle. During the down times, the focus shifted to cost reduction. I was tasked with taking $1 million out of fab costs during such a cycle. So, how to do this? One big thing was to change from time-based maintenance to unit based or predictive maintenance. This saved a significant amount of Maintenance labor (overtime), and Spare parts usage. Another was to decommission low performing equipment, such as on Photocell, to save machine and labor costs. A third was a reduction in replacing spares, which was an $800k per year expense. Finally, we reduced material costs, such as test wafers and Photoresist, to more accurately reflect the current volume. The savings wound up be $1.2 million a year, and the up cycle began again. More on this is in the PM section later.

TPM Appendices

Appendix 1: CEDAC
Appendix 2: Impact Control Matrix
Appendix 3: Action plan with Red, Yellow, Green
Appendix 4: Star points. There are both task and team star
                points.
Appendix 5: Activity Board
Appendix 6: Kanban Board
Appendix 7: Kanban Card.

Step 3: Stacked bar Chart: This a first level breakdown of the first level causes of the loss theme. For example, Idle time could be stacked into No work and No Operator, and Unplanned Downtime into the type and cause of loss. If two themes are chosen, there would be two charts.

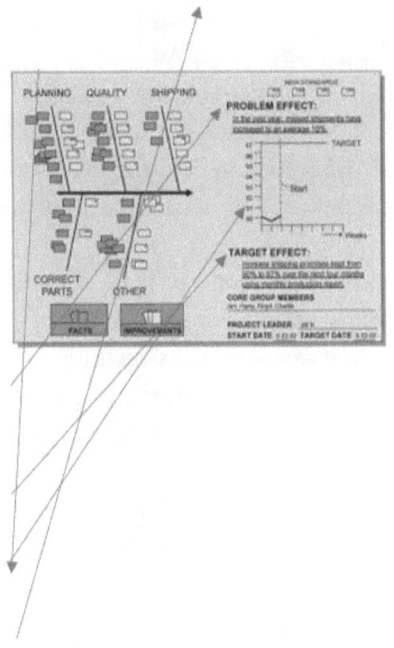

Step 1: Problem Effect Statement. This describes the problem and it's more strategic effect. For example, 25 hour per week of idle time, causes a loss of Production of 2700 units, worth $14,000 in Production.

Step 2: Target Effect: Typically, "half-life" reduction, by when, (13 weeks), as measured by (very important) loss log report.

Step 3: Stacked bar Chart: This a first level breakdown of the first level causes of the loss theme. For example, Idle time could be stacked into No work and No Operator, and Unplanned

Downtime into the type and cause of loss. If two themes are chosen, there would be two charts.

Step 4: Cause of Problem. Yellow Post It Notes are used for the cause side. This answer "Why is there this loss?" It is best to do this in silence, separately writing cards, then discussing them as a group. Causes are categorized by area, by default Man, Method, Materials, Machine, Management and Other. 5 Why is then applied to each yellow card, in an attempt to get to the root cause. These are also yellow cards, placed to the left of the original card.

Step 5: Preventative Solutions, or Ideas: These are blue Post it notes, also silently brain stormed, as a group. Emphasize that there is no idea not worthy of consideration. Allow this process to continue to 20 minutes. Place the blue notes on the chart, next to the problem that the idea helps or resolves.

Step 6: Prioritize Ideas, Use the Impact/ Control Matrix for this step. It can easily be drawn on a Flipchart. (See appendix)

The quadrants are 1: High Impact, High Control, meaning it makes a big difference, and is relatively easy to do, by the team. 2: High Impact, Low control. Makes a big difference, but is hard to do, or needs significant help from outside the team. 3: Low Impact, High Control. Doesn't make a big difference, but relatively easy to do. 4.Low Impact, low control. Small Difference, hard to do. Allow team members to place, and move the cards individually, and then discuss and agree as a team.

Step 7: Select ideas for implementation. Pick the ideas the team would like to try and implement. Clearly, Quadrant 1 ideas are likely to be picked, along with some Q2 and Q3 ideas. About eight or ten should be selected.

Step 8: Develop an Action Plan. This is the typical Who, What, When, Impact format, familiar to Action Planning Formats. Add Red, Yellow, Green macros to indicate late actions, plans in trouble and okay. Update weekly. Team meetings become Action Plan follow ups after about the first four weeks. Provide Who, what when dates on the action plan.

Star Points: I learned Star points from National Semiconductor. Each team has a set of Task and Team Star points. The intent is to divide the "team work" equally. Team members report at the Team meeting on their Star Points.

Task Star Points

Team Star Points

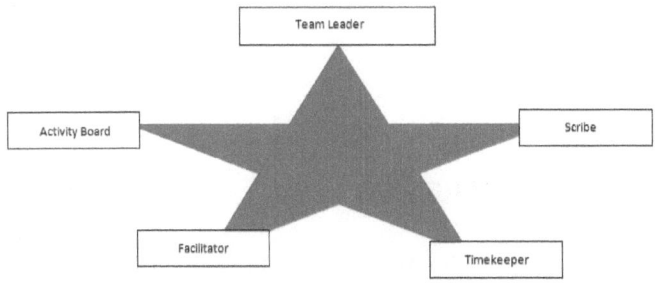

Other TPM Problem Solving Methodologies.

Additional problem methodologies have been employed by TPM practitioners for more complex technical problems. These include P-M analysis, A-3, and Speed Loss analysis. These advanced tools are probably best saved for later TPM cycles.

Other things than TPM in Semiconductor.

Although TPM was the primary focus for Lean in the Semiconductor industry, it wasn't the only thing. At Xerox, I built and implemented the first known Fab pull system, outside of Fab 59, and later refined and improved by Texas Instruments. I also did an ABC cost model, showing how volume of wafers affected unit costs. I worked on SPC chart rationalization, over 400 in the Fab at the time, only about 30 that controlled anything. We reduced this to a more meaningful number, freeing up Process Engineers for improvement work. Team development was also another important development point, working together in cross functional teams, was, at that time, rather new to the highly technical, engineered Fab environment. Developing a "TPM Culture" remained elusive, but positive steps were taken. Teams were empowered, decisions were trusted at lower levels, and cross functional teamwork improved/

How to Screw up TPM

Here are some of the most common errors I have observed from my experience with TPM.

1. Focus on the OEE, not the losses. This is leadership error that must be avoided.

   Measure OEE, but don't make it the sole project purpose. Improve OEE **by reducing equipment losses.**

2. Use Availability x Performance Efficiency x Rate of Quality to define OEE. I've not seen an accurate measure of Performance Efficiency, and it doesn't help define losses.

3. Make it an add on task for people on the teams. EI team members need 4-6 hours a week to work the project and SGA members 2-4 hours. This is a significant amount of resources that must be addressed.

4. Don't involve operators. Make it a Maintenance project.

5. Use computer or "virtual communication" instead of visual, e.g. Activity Boards, Dots, Watermarks, etc.

6. Don't use effective project management methods, including what to do if items become late.

7. For Leadership, forget to ask, "How can I help?"

8. Running a nonproductive team meeting. Focus on "Red" events, not meeting plan. Do not allow ego stroking or deflecting blame in these processes. Facilitate equal roles and participation in meetings, a "parallel operation" no matter what your position is in the organization. There may be an organization hierarchy, but in team activity, all are equal.

A story: Acquisitions:

This is an amusing story that has nothing to do with Lean, other than maybe commenting on the difficulty of company acquisitions into a Lean culture. The company I was working for had acquired two other companies that, apparently, needed to be indoctrinated into the "culture" of the acquiring company. I'm not sure anybody knew what the that meant, but I was asked to accompany the VP of Ops to an Ohio facility to explain this. Although Lean and TPM were only 18 months old, it was apparently accepted as being part of the acquiring company's culture. So, I was asked to come in to explain Lean and TPM to the staff. So, the VP of Ops got to the main entrance and asked for the Plant Manager. I noticed the VP of Ops, Joe, become, more and more upset and agitated as he waited. While we were waiting, I noticed the previously companies' logo, Sparky the dog, prominently displayed in the lobby. The Plant Manager showed up, and the VP, red veins in his neck prominently displayed, shouted, "You have 30 minutes to get that fxxxxing dog out of this lobby, or I'll find someone who will." I tried to suppress my laughter and when we left that night, Sparky was gone. It didn't change any culture, but it did make some kind of point, I suppose.

CHAPTER FIVE
SEMICONDUCTOR WORK AS AN EMPLOYEE

Introduction International Rectifier and Allied Signal

Frankly I was tired of the road, and six months out of the year with international travel. So, craving something more local and permanent.

Fortunately, an old friend and colleague of mind, contacted me, and asked me if I could help. Hussein Naguib had given me my first consulting job at his fab in LA, and later hired me at his site in Arlington, Texas. He had originally met me a conference, in which I presented a paper on TPM. The position was full time, rather than as a consultant, and was based in Temecula, California. The fab operation had 17 primary languages spoken. How to train and reinforce in such and environment, was the question. "A picture is worth a thousand words" is an apt adage here. We stated writing hundreds of "One Point Lessons", another key TPM and Lean tool, to supplement Fab written specs and procedures. But there continued to be Quality issues. I was asked to lead a team to investigate and solve the problem. The yield was 88% and needed to be 94%. As those of you in the industry are aware, throwing away a wafer is very costly. So, what was going on?

One thing that came up quickly was the fab was expanding business rapidly, which required hiring many new workers. The thought was the yield loss was hurt because of all of the new people. Not a good assumption, the data proved. I did a study that related fab human caused defects to experience level, and found almost perfect negative correlation, e.g. the more experienced the operator, the more mistakes they made. This was surprising to me, as well as Fab leadership. After further investigation, it was revealed that more experienced operators "knew what they were doing", and tended not to follow specs, one point lessons, or quality alerts, whereas new people would do so more to follow the documentation, particularly the OPL's (One Point Lessons) with key Quality points. Supervisors were told to retrain all employees on specs, OPL's and Yield loss and reinforced insistence on following the documents. Several documents needed to be updated based on this reinforcement, which was a good thing. This countermeasure got us part of the way there, but something else was needed. Once again surprisingly, (prepare to be surprised a lot in this book), the answer lay in the shift pattern.

For many years, the Fab had worked a 5-2-2-5 shift pattern, which means five days on, two days off, two days on and five days off. This worked well for the employees, many of which used the five day off time for second jobs or small business work. Studying the data, we found that more errors were made on the first day back from five days off, than at every other time, a statistically relevant difference. It took a while, and some concessions to the workforce, but we managed to change the shift pattern to 4-3-3-4, and the Quality took an uptick from this.

Finally, Quality circles were introduced to Fab teams, with weekly meetings held to discuss losses and quality measures binned to their area. The training department facilitated these meetings. After 6 months, Fab yield had improved to 94%, due to these countermeasures, and perhaps the Placebo effect, but mission accomplished.

Then because it was a Fab, it was on to equipment and TPM. We went right to the TOC process and decided to start with Ion Implanters, it seems always to be the Ion Implanters. The team was formed and led by the Equipment Engineering Manager. He was technically astute, but as is common, human relations deficient.

He and I argued constantly about OEE, losses and Actions, but eventually we became good team players and colleagues. One of the main contentions was about a "Required Loss" and a "non-required loss. This was a common argument over the years. In his view, as many think, SPC Checks, Planned Downtime, Setup, etc. are not losses, because they needed to be done. This was opposed to TPM, which argues that anytime equipment is not running product at optimal speed is a loss. Further, Slow Speed was not a loss in his view, as slowing down the machine to better ensure quality was not a loss, but a benefit. Again, to TPM, a loss is a loss, with the intention of reducing it. So, do you speed up a machine and incur more yield loss? Of course not, but perhaps, as in most things, there is reasonable middle ground. Semiconductor people are trained that yield is everything, and their objectives and performance reviews and KPI's are largely based on Yield improvements. To modify this to a more "balanced score card", was and continues to be, an important cultural change. The good news was, all of these above points were openly discussed and debated in the team, not just arbitrarily decided by Engineering. A very good thing.

Then, I got involved with securing training funding from the State of California. They were concerned that jobs were fleeing the state for cheaper labor places, both in the US and abroad. So, they encouraged companies to train and retrain employees in key industries, especially in high technology, to retain jobs. After tons of paperwork, we were awarded $440k to train the workforce on TPM and other Lean tools. It was of huge value to a medium sized company.

A word about Leadership. Hussein Naguib was a great and inspirational Leader, one of the best I have known. It was with regret I left them but was highly recruited by some national consulting companies. My 12-year career had always been solo, so it was time to see what the larger consulting world had to offer.

Consulting and the Consulting world.

So, I suppose it's time for my rant about consultants. My original mentor taught me, "those who can't do, teach, those who can't teach consult". Basically, don't listen to us. I was a consultant for 12 years on my own, and always prided myself as being the "non consultant consultant", choosing to become deeply involved in the processes of fewer clients. The thing to understand about the national consulting companies, and of course there are exceptions, is that it's all about billable hours, rather than helping the clients. Of course, they would never own up to that, and I don't even claim it to be true, just my experience. My early experience was tainted by the "Speed is Life" firms that valued cycle time over everything. They typically rely on one size fits all recipes for doing things and have inflated and wafer thin (pun intended) resumes about Lean experiences and success.

And then there are the "TPS Gurus", who do a bunch of Kaizen events groups, notable in the industry. I always advise, find your own path, not someone else's.

Even if you get the acclaimed experts, such a JIPM from Japan, funny things happen. A client was implementing a companywide TPM effort and hired me to help. They also contracted with JIPM to come in and inspect its plants. The long-awaited visit by the "expert" occurred, and we were all instructed to follow him around, and write down everything he said, by the way, which was in Japanese, which none of us understood. He was also wired for sound, so that all other could hear his words of wisdom. During a break, the expert went to the bathroom and did speak through the microphone in a language everyone could understand…tinkle, tinkle, tinkle. I don't remember anything else about the business, or any wisdom he may have imparted, but I do remember the tinkles.

So, I was quite careful in choosing my next set of experiences. There were two interested companies, both with a good client list, and with assurances that I could do my, rather than their thing. I first went to work as the "technical rep" for the first company, going along with the Sales guy to pitch the work from a process view. It wasn't long before we got our first client, of course, in the Semiconductor industry. I showed up for work, on the opening Monday, and much to my chagrin, there were four other consultants joining me, only one of which had any experience in Semiconductor, and most of which had a shallow or mistaken view of Lean and TPM. In fact, none of them knew much about equipment or process. Mostly managers from other companies who had people do the Lean work for them. The work was the same as I did solo, so I questioned the need for such a large team. I was told the billable hours story, and the gullible client was told the progress would be faster with a larger team. This lasted a year, and the effort, albeit successful, was deemed too expensive, and was not continued. Most of my time, as the lead, was spent teaching the team about equipment and wafers, how to do real Lean, and picking up for them when they made inevitable process mistakes.

So, the next interested company was still interested, and had landed a contract with major electronics (though not

Semiconductor) firm, interested in improving Manufacturing. Again, in a 400-person plant, a team of five people was needed to consult. I managed to get a knowledgeable friend and sharp Industrial Engineer, but the others were non experienced or out of their expertise for what we were doing. One was a "Human resource" expert to help with the people side. The company was also big into "Six Sigma", as well as Lean, and had just spent a bunch of money and resources to do "Green Belt" training, so they were theoretically well equipped to help us. Gains were marginal, and we left after 6 months. Lean before 6 Sigma (if ever 6 Sigma) because reducing variation in a variable and unstable process, without the involvement of people, is an expensive waste of time. Same story, different verse.

More consulting experiences:

I'm hired for a variety of companies, for a variety of reasons. However, I've never been good at Marketing and Promotion. So, during this phase of relying on Consulting companies for leads and work, I had some interesting experiences. Also, my solo gigs also provided some learning insights. Described below are a few:

1. Oil and Gas industry- The consulting company was invited in to get Continuous Improvement started. The Oklahoma factory was at full production and needed more output. So, I and a team of four went in for a six-month engagement. As usual, the other team members were Lean and industry inexperienced, but meant more billable hours. We were brought in because a new VP, who had come from a Lean company saw the benefits and knew he needed help. In the opening meeting, he talked about us, the

consultants, as "The Borg", and said, "Resistance was futile". But as is normal, resistance was out there are ready to battle. The biggest resistance was from the "MRP camp". They had recently implemented a new system, were struggling with it for the usual reasons, but still believed in it, with an almost religious fervor. Then, I started talking about doing pull systems, and dismantling significant parts of the system, which was blasphemy for them. We did a pilot with pull, and was successful, which got the "MRP'ers", even more worried. We agreed to a tepid compromise, and shortly thereafter left the engagement. I don't know what happened with the systems dilemma, but it was a long and arduous battle between the MRP/ERP systems, and Lean/Pull, and this is not the space for those arguments. But I ran into this controversy many times in my career, with varying degrees of resolution.

2. Plastic Injection Molding. In a major supplier Iowa plant, I was invited to assess their CI effort, as they had been at it for a while, and now in their own works, stuck. A new VP of Ops was hired and was a big Lean proponent. So, somehow, they found me. During my initial assessment tour, I wandered into a Quality Circle meeting, where the discussion of a new storage bin they were making for Wal Mart. Several Quality improvement suggestions were made, and then the Project leader interjected, "You people don't understand, Wal Mart doesn't want a Quality Storage Bin, it costs too much". Going into some detail, he described Wal Mart was willing to pay $8 for a low-quality bin. A defect free bin would cost $14, which the customer wouldn't pay for. The discussion of how to make a higher quality product at a lower

cost, wasn't part of this companies Lean discussion. Nor was inventory, which was everywhere. Batch sizing forecast driven systems, and inefficiency had driven inventory levels to unacceptable levels. Again, this was not a part of the CI discussion which was primarily Kaizen based. Management listened to my frank observations in the closing meeting, which was peppered with comments of "Hopefully that will get better". The VP of Ops then said something I'll never forget. "Hope is not a method" he said, "Tell me what you're going to do about it, not what your hopes are". Words to live by.

3. Toyota Supplier

Injection molding- I seemed to be getting into injection molding back then. My colleague and I were hired to go into an Indiana plant, as Toyota was complaining that the two hours direct to line deliveries truck were not always full, and their production was threatened to be disrupted.

So, we show up, and were ushered into a conference room with corporate executives. We were informed that all of the Plant Senior Management had quit, down to the Supervisor level and my colleague and I would "have to run the plant for a while". As it was a 24-hour operation, this meant my partner and I would have to work 12-hour shifts, and attend to plant, as well as Lean duties. The injection molding process had 42% baseline OEE's, with significant losses in Setup Time, Rework Time, Minor Stoppages and Downtime. As previously observed, Pull Systems, such as Toyota had implemented could not be supported without effective equipment.

Speaking of customer required pull systems, a story comes to mind. In one of my Semiconductor plants. I was told that a major automotive customer was "implanting pull" for all major suppliers, and I needed to do this for a backend semiconductor plant. I got a bit nosy and found out what that meant was for us to deliver daily rates to an automotive customer warehouse, where the product would sit for 2-6 weeks. This is classic "Lean malpractice", but we had to play along, and make linear deliveries to the warehouse. So, Linearity did improve, but it certainly wasn't pull. Of course, the cost of this warehouse was to be borne by us, the supplier. Discussions about to direct to plant deliveries went nowhere although our automotive line was perfectly capable of supporting it.

4. In my solo consulting life, there are stories as well. I was invited into an Aerospace plant in Southern California to review and access their Lean work. Turns out, they wanted validation more than assessment. Keep this in mind, as a Lean consultant or internal resource. My assessment, over a six-week period, contained three key points.

    a. Don't mix up Lean and Six Sigma. They had spent hundreds of thousands of dollars training and certifying Green Belts, and all they did was work on Lean Projects. The processes do not merge well together and shouldn't be the approach. Do Lean first.

    b. Don't force improvement with Management reviews. The company had an elaborate system of checking CI progress and seeing if results were being met. There was no protocol of "how can I help", only corrective action, and all at the high levels, mostly punitive and personal on people who were not achieving results.

c. Supermarkets are for grocery stores. The corporate CI director had gotten into his mind the Supermarkets were the most effective way dealing with process imbalances, rather than working on the imbalances themselves. I found the Supermarkets little more than a relabeling of WIP warehouses, albeit on the floor. I expressed my opinion to plant Leadership and "green belts" and was roundly criticized for "not following the company recipe". Again, we are not baking bread or replicating Toyota's Post WW2 experience, we are trying to implement sustainable improvement. So, my suggestions were noted, and quickly discarded. Time to move on.

I feel it necessary to say that there are excellent top-notch firms out there. One of them is mentioned below.

So, for me, it was back to the drawing board about how to help companies. Title and position didn't matter but fit and ability to contribute did. So, onto the next chapter.

Lessons from this Experience

1. Be very careful using consultants. Use someone you know or has been recognized by a colleague.
2. Be sure the Consultants Lean vision matches yours. Be sure it includes Tools, Culture and Leadership
3. Be sure it includes Strategic, not just tactical planning.

4. Identify an internal resource to take over for the consultants, as soon as possible. Find an internal resource who "gets it". Linda Miller or Sherry Wilkes.
5. Don't listen to anybody who wants to do Six Sigma or train green belts.
6. Don't hire a consultant(s) who tells you they can reduce costs with Lean. It is not about that but may be a natural outcome of an implementation.
7. Don't hire Lean/Six Sigma hybrid companies, do Lean first.
8. Listen to your advisors, but not too literally.

    If this seems to eliminate many/most consulting firms, it's probably true. However, again there are some good ones out there that can help launch and continue the process.

Windows and Doors

I was called by a guy who made GM seat belts in Kansas City. I wanted to experience Lean as an insider, rather than a consultant. Finally, I wanted to experience Continuous Improvement as an insider, rather than a Consultant, although I never though of myself as one, branding myself as the "Non consultant consultant". Needing to be more of a part of, I suppose. So, I made the trip to Southwest Missouri to view an architectural Window and Door plant, with 1200 employees and lots of business. I have to admit to someone of a shock from what I saw. From the somewhat obsessive organization of High tech, I observed organized chaos in this plant. The New VP of Ops from the Seatbelt plants was hired to implement Lean, as he had done it in a previous plant, but like many leaders, didn't really grasp the details. He had heard of me, somewhere, and asked me to give him an assessment. My response was, "I don't know if I can help here, it's pretty out of control". He appealed to my need for a challenge, and besides, I thought anything I could do would help. So, I agreed, for the first time in 12 years, to be an employee, and went to work. But, where to start? I was taught somewhere, to always start with the customer. So, what did the customers think? Internally, the organization thought everything was fine, and had the metrics to prove it. Talking to customers painted a completely different picture.

The Illusion of Metrics

So, part of my process is to dig deeply into the data. Why did the company think they were on time, when the customers thought otherwise? The metric criteria provided the answer, Internally, the company measured the amount of sales order items delivered to the company's promised dates. This number was 96%. The problems was the customers needed the material delivered in a certain sequence, e.g. the metal to put the windows and doors into, needed to be there and installed before anything could be installed. And the 4% the company was late on was the subframe metal. Plus, the company's promise date differed widely from the customer need date, due to restrictions and constraints put on by the ERP system. More on that later. Actual on Time delivery, as measured by 100% of the material delivered by the customer need date was 6%. This was the problem that needed to be solved. Work on the right problem. Management was stunned and in denial of this data but did accept something needed to be done. So, I went to work getting Sub Frame on time. Sub frame had a schedule that was totally disconnected to customer needs, so we adjusted that, so that the most important work was worked on first. This was a tedious, manual process at first, but we were aided by an IT group that intuitively grasped the wisdom of our approach. We then applied the TPM approach to the equipment, Metal cutting and shaping, and made gains. Parallel to this, we formed a Cross Functional Team composed of all levels and sections of the organizations to solve the "On Time Delivery" issue. 50 people showed up to the first meeting, in part because they didn't understand it, in part because Senior Management insisted on it, in Part to protect their ass, to make sure they weren't blamed for the problem. If any of this sounds familiar, just nod your head and keep reading, Typical organization dynamics. We quickly winnowed the team down to 12 key members and went into the Problem-Solving process. Cross functional miscommunication and siloes quickly came to the surface. Solving these became a longer-term solution. Focus on getting the customer what they need what they need it. Get Subframe on time. Deliver subframe specs to manufacturing as soon as possible. Make products needed, rather than product that can't be turned into sales anyway, because of problems with other areas. Produce more in Subframe by becoming more efficient. It was the first time in the history of the company departments had worked together for a common goal, and it was powerful. Within three months, we had gotten the "real" OTD number up to 65%, and eventually to the high 80%'s. Culturally, it taught the organization the power of working together, and solving problems collectively. This is also where I met Sherry Wilkes, and operator in the Subframe department. Part of our training was to run a simulation of how a push system worked, as opposed to our proposed pull system. All operators from Sub Frame were invited. Sherry came with her team in the Push system example, and then we took a break to convert the line. Sherry wanted to know if she could ask a question, and I said sure. Sherry then asked why we didn't do it another way and went on to perfectly describe the pull system we were about to demonstrate. I remember asking myself, "who is this person", and continued with the simulation. Sherry had an intuitive grasp of Lean and Pull systems that can't be trained. Find these people in your organization and use them on your project team. Sherry became my first Lean employee, and today manages the Lean Planning group. I appointed her to lead the Subframe effort, and she diligently and wisely led her department into being on time, with the right products at the right time. Her product knowledge proved invaluable. Her only previous job had been in a greenhouse, and she helped start and grow Lean at this plant. She helped introduce the software to segregate "producible" for "non producible" work, which became a key Lean methodology.

Next, I moved to our Extrusion process. I moved here because they were basically too efficient. They were producing too much aluminum, which went into inventory, and there was a capital project for a third warehouse full of aluminum. My boss asked if I could find a way to avoid buying this warehouse and reduce the large inventory cost.

They produced hundreds of tons of extruded metal weekly, the metric was how much can be produced, rather than how much can be turned into Product. A big change. It took a long time to change the culture from, "the more we make the better", to can we make it when the downstream process requires it". Don't underestimate the culture change required to do this.

The current process was to have 6 week "MRP order launch signals", which authorized 6 weeks of a run of metal, with no visibility if it could be supported by any other parts of the Production process. We started with TPM, to improve the ability to changeover and set up more quickly. The Extrusion manger was understandably reluctant, and he had always been measured on Pounds of Metal produced, and this clearly needed to change. We discussed one day pull signals, and we agreed on a three-month delay to work on Setup up time. We identified 38 hours a week of setup time and used QCO and Setup reduction protocols to work on it. Much of this involved separating internal and external setup time, and having dies "close, clean and ready". The basics. Part of this involved reorganized the die racks, based on usage. There were over 2000 dies in the racks, over half which had been not used for over two years. High volume dies were moved closer to the cleaning tanks. Die cleaning procedures and a faster cleaning chemical were used to speed up the process. After one EI cycle, the Setup loss was reduced to 9 hours per week.

We then reduced the pull signal from MRP from six weeks to three weeks, then finally to three days. Extrusion production dropped by 20%, but it was the right die at the right time, where it could be used by a downstream process, overtime in Extrusion was reduced by half. I tried to get a one day pull signal, but the Extrusion Manger, who was a good friend, thought that was going a bit far. I took the 80% inventory reduction, the saving of the third warehouse, and most importantly, introducing pull and the awareness and importance of downstream process to the factory as major improvements.

So, at this point, I had earned some "organizational credibility". So, what to do next. I decided to expand the pull system approach, used effectively in Extrusion, to the rest of the process. But, a couple of things happened in the meantime. First, I was promoted to Plant Manager, then Director of Operations, with the theory that I would have less resistance because I was in charge. In fact, nothing could be further from the truth. More on that later. For now, my job was to fire the two current plant managers, both good guys, but not Lean people, to further the process. This was a painful, but necessary experience. Secondly, top Leadership determined that I needed "help", in the form of bringing in outside resources to help develop lean. I opposed this, and wanted a small Lean team, composed of Plant people who understood the intricacies and specifics of the process. Two fallacies here, both lessons learned. One, resistance fades when you are in charge, and two, help of the wrong sort actually helps.

But Leadership decided to bring in five recent Wichita State MBA's- who knew Lean from a "book", but not a practical standpoint. I immediately found the leader of this group to be a "player", with a limited level of knowledge. But he had a program and a plan, and it was quite aligned to the "recipe" defined in school. The problem was it had no basis in practicality. I allowed them to do a pilot project, and I must admit, knowing it would fail. And it did, rather spectacularly. The lessons are, don't rely on outside "experts", and rely on internal experts, who are lean "learnable" to implement the process. This team dispersed quickly, and I formed my own Lean team, composed of process experts who were teachable,

The other problem was the high level of esteem the MRP led Production and Planning organization held. There was a VP level position, who had spearheaded the MRP/ERP implementation. He was a powerful voice in the organization, and reluctant to let go of authority. He saw what I was doing and was cautiously supportive. I worked for three months, with IT and my internal team to develop an EFFlow app, that would effectively develop pull signals from one process to the next. The organizational arguments were long and heated, but eventually, I was successful in getting this done. The Friday before the weekend implementation, I got a call from my boss, explaining to me that this was a "career limiting activity" if it failed. It did not fail and was a huge success.

EFFlow

The premise or the system is a simple one. Don't make anything upstream for a product, unless downstream processes can support it. For this plant, this meant not making any Windows and Doors that did not have Glass availability, which was suffering from Widespread shortages. We needed to turn off the Order Generation and Release part of the ERP system, as it seemed to not recognize this simple fact. Changing Due dates was a non-manageable task, we put in an electronic pull system that separated "Producible from Non-Producible" work, and "unschedule" upstream demands to the requirement. A lean cell planning team was launched to replace the planners and schedulers of the current process. The skill sets of these people were quite different from the traditional planners and schedulers. Process, rather than MRP experts. We developed area schedules to support producible products. Production volume and productivity rose, and departments made only producible products. EFFlow was an electronic pull system, linked with a system that separated producible and non-producible work. Outside produced glass was the main shortage, and nothing was produced until a firm promise for delivery was given. The impact on inventory and WIP were dramatic. It did not produce the nonresistance that leadership thought it would. If anything, resistance was more open and vocal, which was a good thing. The impact on inventory and WIP were dramatic, but we still had to keep the Production numbers up.

A work about resources. The town in SW Missouri had 6000 people and 8000 jobs, and the plant was facing a 30% increase in production. There were simply no people to hire, so the increase had to be dealt with improved Productivity. Again, metrics and behavior were our constraint. The production metric was sales order volume, and Production supervisors would "cherry pick" their Production schedule for the easy work, and leave the low dollar, harder work behind. Also, schedule delivery would be secondary to dollars produced, and the culture changes to effect these changes were dramatic and huge. But the team and I found a way. Implementing and old CI concept called "Linearity" was also very helpful. The plant was practicing a typical "Hockey stick" production, where at the end of the week, and especially the month, was raised to "make the numbers". My original mentor, John Costanza had taught me the concept of Linearity, which means "make the daily rate every day". See chart below. Measure Linearity deviations. It's kind of like OEE for process flow. So, at this plant, I was looking at the extreme "hockey stick production" we were experiencing. Gathering data, I noticed that 60% of the month's production was made the last week of the month, and 40% the last two days. Applying the Linearity deviation formula, I had learned, I saw our linearity was 4%. Asking the "so what" question produced the following.

1. We cleaned out the system at the end of the month, leaving empty lines, and nothing to do at the beginning of the next month
2. We spent money on overtime and other costs to push production out at the end of the month.
3. We disrupted the pull system, which was largely predicated on linear production.

4. Upstream processes were even more drastically affected by nonlinear production.

5. Customer performance was negatively impacted.

So, I started measuring my Production managers and supervisors on Linearity, a vast departure from the previous measure of simply making the monthly sales number. This is a culture change that was significant and time consuming, and not without casualties. Eventually, we got the Linearity measure up to 65%, and production flowed more efficiently and smoothly.

Leadership insisted I needed help, as I was running a plant and leading the CI effort. "Help" then arrived in the form of an assistant plant manager, whose first work, was to implement a "Mr. Clean" activity on the glazing lines. These lines, largely populated by Guatemalan immigrants, liked to chew sunflower seeds, and sometimes spit them on the floor. The Assistant Plant Manager decided on the Mr. Clean program, which included large posters of the bald product guy, on each line, with an inspirational slogan, which most of the workers did not understand. My much less nuanced way of handling the situation was to go out to line talk to the workers, tell them to dispose of the seeds responsibly, and put additional waste bins on each line. No data exists for whose approach worked better, but I have my thoughts.

But there were "bigger fish to fry". We tried a new approach with reorganizing glazing lines to not be product, but more process focused, so that a line could produce multiple products. We also tried to "Mix Model Sequence" products through a line, to effect maximum flow. Both of these pilots of advanced Lean techniques had mixed results, the first due to employee specific skill training, the second due to changes needed to the pull system and had limited success. But it worked with persistence and adherence to principles.

We then moved on to plant security. The plant was losing over $250k per year in lost drills, tools, and other items. Lean suggested "Shadow boards", where the tools were displayed, with outlines, in the work area, rather than in locked in individual toolboxes. The town in SW Missouri was small, and one day, I wandered into a downtown Pawn Shop. Imaging my surprise upon seeing dozens of plant drills, with the asset number scratched off. So, we tried Shadow boards, quickly seeing missing places for tools on the Shadow boards. We had to put plastic see through guards with locks over the shadow boards, with access only to the Supervisors. I felt bad about not trusting the employees and decided to investigate further. Also, Management decided to buy a $85,000 Security camera system, to be deployed throughout the plant. This was a dismal failure, as the cameras had nowhere near the resolution to determine who did a theft, and it completely angered the employees. I decided to stay in my car one night, at the rear Extrusion door, and see if I could determine what was going on. And, much to my surprise, it was the Security Guards who were doing the theft! Culprits apprehended, cameras removed, but damage done. And, by the way, there was a Meth Lab delivery at the same gate.

HR Initiatives at the Plant.

1. Asking Employees what they needed. I made my way around the 1200-person plant, department by department, and met with the people and asked what they needed from me. I was told by some that this was the first time they had ever seen a member of senior

management and told by many others I was the first one to ask them what they needed. The number one answer we needed was a Saturday off, which they hadn't had in months. The plant had experienced a 30% increase in volume, and being in a rural location, had trouble finding people. But I needed a "win" with them and said I would promise that by the end of the next month. I was confident the Lean improvements started would pay off but wasn't sure how quickly they would sustain. This was the first of many things I didn't tell my boss about, as he would have said, "just make sure you make your numbers". Well, in week 7 after the meetings were conducted, I announced a plant wide Saturday off. There was a new Wal Mart in town, and of course, I met many of the employees in the store. I was met by a family, who just wanted to thank me for the extra time off to spend with their small children. This made it all worth it for me. But I was taught an axiom a long time ago that "No good deed with go unpunished". As the Lean activities grew and took root, less and less Saturdays were needed, and after a few months, Saturday overtime was rare. And of course, people would now complain about missing the overtime, and needing money to make ends meet. "No good deed will go unpunished"

2. The true spirit of Kaizen, not "event mentality". I wanted employee ideas to be heard, so I convened a supervisory management team to gather and discuss employee ideas for improvement.

At first, the silence was deafening. They just weren't used to being asked their opinion. Finally, I put some rules in. Every idea, no matter how small, large, silly or trivial, would be discussed by the eight-person leadership team, and a member would get back to to the employee within 72 hours. The first meeting after this yielded 40 suggestions and lasted six hours. The members were mostly dismissive of the suggestions, but mostly to drive the cultural change, I insisted on the side of implementing them if possible. Two years later, over $200k in cost savings had been realized by the program. By the way, this is the true idea of "Kaizen", not the five-day event.

3. Gainsharing. I promised a lot of things to the employees during my three plus year stint. One of the most controversial was offering a Gainsharing package to the employees, once we became profitable. It seemed pretty "Pie in the Sky" at the time, as we were losing $1.2 million each year. This is probably why the executives approved it. But after the second year, we were marginally profitable, and in the third year, we made $6.8 million. So, we had an employee meeting to tell them we were going to share in the profits. The hard part was the distribution methodology, which I worked out in conjuncture with HR. It was to be a flat payout to each employee, based on number of hours worked. Supervisors, but not managers were to be included. The payout was a few hundred dollars, and again we return to the theme of "No Good Dead Shall Go Unpunished". Supervisors, who were salaried, were incensed, in that they made no overtime hour bump, as some hourly employees did, even as overtime was significantly reduced. We gave the Supervisors an extra $50, and everyone seemed happy.

4. HR Lean Group. I was a Manufacturing guy, but other areas became interested in learning more about this process. Although to many "Lean HR", may

seem to be an oxymoron, I was fortunate to have a group that wanted to work on solving problems. We were having problems around the administration of the attendance policy and decided to form a cross functional team to address it. Over a 13-week cycle a fairer more equitable policy was adopted that was agreeable to all. It was critical to have hourly employees on the team and have their agreement. It was a non-union operation.

Sales and Operational Planning Process

We continued to experience problems with the front end of the S and OP (Sales and Operational Planning System). We had largely shut off the back end with the pull systems and EFFlow but needed to improve how promise dates were given to customers. The As-Is was to put the nearest date the system showed capacity, and offer that to the customer as a promise. Customers, being quite smart, put in orders early to procure a sooner delivery date, oftentimes with final product specs and engineering not being completed. Also, the system had a hard time recognizing changes in capacity, understanding that the plant had greater capacity and flexibility than before. We put a filter in the system that required the customer to have Engineering complete before a date could be assigned, and had a monthly meeting to discuss what could be done for jobs that fell outside the customer required date, based on the system capacity. Oftentimes, Production had innovative and creative solutions to making these dates possible, and over time, customers stopped putting jobs in early to "save their place in line".

Results of Lean at the Plant- Wins and Losses

The "wins" speak for themselves and are outlined above. For me personally, it was the people and culture development that spoke most clearly, the Sherry Wilkes of the operation, the change in the Employee culture. The at least partially changing the culture from a top down, do as I say culture, to a least a semi participative one. I would have liked to take this further but ran out of time. I am also grateful for support departments like IT, HR, Finance and S and OP to step up to the process, when they realized there were issues, and they could contribute to the solution. And, the production and financial benefits speak for themselves.

Now, let's get to the losses, because that's where the learning comes from. The Design Engineering handoff to production process was flawed, with bad communication of handoffs, and an incomplete understanding that if it can be made in a lab, it may not be mass producible in Production. I tried to drive improvements in this process but was not successful. All parties were too invested in their siloed process, and top management was not willing to intervene.

Which brings us to the next problem. Management vs. Leadership. This, frankly, did not change at this company. While Management was happy with the results of the Lean process, they did not associate it with anything they had to do differently, and I didn't strongly enough push it. We did try some Strategic Planning (Hoshins), but quickly deteriorated into management posturing and defending. I later learned that I didn't know how to manage the process.

Leadership was also unable and/or unwilling to change any of their behavior to support the process. Again, my fault. We did have a Steering Committee, but no GEMBA walks, Lean Leadership training, or teaching moments where they could have made a difference. But, live and learn and move on. Under the precept of "No Good Deed will go unpunished", our financial turnaround meant we were ripe for acquisition, and we were acquired by a larger corporation, who had a different understanding of what Continuous Improvement that I did. So, it was time to move on.

Changing the metrics also was a challenging task that never got resolved. I got a call from my Traffic Manager one day, who wanted to inform me that my boss, the VP, had informed him to do something. Because of Production improvements, we went from behind schedule to ahead of schedule, but could not let the shipment numbers suffer. So, we went to "trucks on the hill" approach. We would ship the product, instead of to the customer, to a truck, which would be stored on a hill alongside the plant, until the customer wanted it. I walked back to the "hill" one day and counted the trucks full of product. There were over 100. The traffic manager informed me the VP wanted to ship them to an offsite holding yard, as they then could be counted as "Sales". My objections went unheard, and the legality of the scam went unnoticed.

I regret two things from this experience. The first is allowing "Hay in the Barn", a rural term meaning keeping things in reserve for when they were needed. We went from being hopelessly behind schedule, to being well ahead. My Production supervisors argued for "hay in the barn", which meant producing a product on Friday, but not reporting it until the following week to improve linearity. I reluctantly complied and wished I hadn't.

The Wood Industry

Personally, I had a decision to make. Did I want to do Lean full time, resume an Operations role, or try to do the dual role? Frankly in a 1200-person plant, it was impossible to do both roles justice, but my thought was that, in a smaller theater, both roles could be enacted. So, a Truss and Wall Panel company in Arizona came along that wanted a Plant Manager that also knew Lean. It only had 120 employees, and top leadership seemed interested, albeit not knowledgeable in the Lean process. So, I accepted the position. Leaning out Production was a straightforward process. There were two Production lines, one to make trusses, and another, a more automated process to make Wall panels. I implemented Visual Controls, Pull, and TPM on the Saws. Wall panel improvements included the download process from Design to Production about what to make, and in the right sequence. These processes took about six months, and then other problems came to the fore. One was the traffic problem. The call from the President said, "Our traffic costs are now higher than our Labor costs, you're the Lean guy, fix it.". So, I got into it with our traffic Supervisors, two highly talented brothers. At this time, gas prices were spiraling, and though our plant was in Yuma, Arizona, most of our customers were in Southern California. Problem solving methods revealed two major issues, non-optimal loading of the trucks and no back hauling available from Southern California. We had a fleet of 16 trucks, so this was a significant problem. We analyzed Truck loading patterns, together with site production schedules, and tare weight lode restrictions, and found about a 20% improvement potential, which we took advantage of. The backhauling from California proved to be stickier problem, who would send product from California to Yuma, but we aggressively pursued backhaul business, and found products such as pallets, that we could send back to Arizona cheaper, as we were already absorbing all the fixed costs. This is was another 25% production in freight costs. So, now the plant costs were relatively under control, and freight and office costs reductions were achieved and had substantially reduced Freight costs. But as always, another problem appeared. This one related to field installation costs. We installed about 65% of our business, including some government projects, where construction workers were paid $47 an hour to install product. Upon site inspection, I noticed up to half of their time was spent trying to find the product in a vast amount of wood that was shipped from the plant. So, the first step was clearly CANDO, organizing the product so the next day's stuff would be most readily available, Then the next, and more difficult step, was to "pull" the product from the plant, so that it wouldn't be shipped until a day or two before needed. This was a difficult problem, as production, freight, and installation requirements needed to be coordinated. But, as usual, people in teams who are empowered work out solutions, albeit manual ones, and that was the case here. Although my production numbers took a bit of a hit, the supply chain costs went down by 30%, keeping up afloat longer than we should have. But then the great housing recession hit, and no amount of Lean work could help us there. Business came to a screeching halt; layoffs began the plant eventually closed.

Lessons from this experience:

1. I failed again to get Management/Leadership involved in the process. Perhaps I hadn't fully learned this yet, or this management team wasn't capable of Lean leadership. Much greater progress could have been made with Leadership Lean training and actions.

2. It's not about just Production. It's about the whole "Supply Chain" experience, including installation and

transportation. Positive actions to one part, can cause larger negative impacts in other areas.

3. Don't tolerate bosses who undermine your authority. The owner would storm in on occasion, walk to line, and come to my office, telling who to fire. I should have known the "handwriting on the wall", and left then, as a leader of integrity, but didn't, in the interest of the people.

4. Lean can't overcome everything. Severe market downturns, such as the recession of 2009, and the current Corona Virus outbreak, are beyond the scope of Lean, although its roots came from a similar desperate situation in Post WW2 Japan. So, perhaps there is a larger lesson here.

So, now, I was jobless again, and looking for a place to work. There was a short consulting stint, at an Aerospace operation in Phoenix, where I was asked to look at their Lean effort. It was entirely Kaizen based, with one five-day event per month scheduled. I attended one event, in which very little time was spent on Lean, but mostly on Training, Value Stream Mapping and the rah-rah Management presentation. The only real improvement suggestion was to transfer and inspection operation downstream to another department. Presenting my findings to Management led to my quick dismissal.

So, I started listening to job offers. I had one from Honeywell, which seemed quite sincere in their CI efforts. I was recruited and hired. On the Friday before my Monday start date, I received a call from the hiring manager, indicating the offer had been withdrawn due to "corporate cutback", so I went back to the drawing board. So, started a long, drawn out recruiting and hiring process by a lumber company in Washington state. Ironically, the hiring process was part of a later Lean effort that this process was later handled and improved by a Lean team.

The company wanted to hire me but had disagreements on my role. Operations wanted a person to start a major Lean effort in the company, but the Sales group wanted a traditional Industrial Engineer to analyze the cost structure, basically to prove Operation costs were too high. I interviewed six times, including three times in person, without resolution. There was continued confusion after my hire, and I took on the dual role of traditional Industrial Engineer and Continuous Improvement leader.

But, first, a short story. I moved to the Seattle/Tacoma area and was put up in a hotel near the plant. I went to work every day and returned to the hotel. After about six weeks, I exited to go to work, looked up into the sky, and there was this huge mountain, Mt. Rainier, which I had not noticed before. It was winter, and the skies were grey for extended periods. Well, I noticed the mountain, and in the plant too, there were mountains to climb. The biggest constraint from a company standpoint were the heated, almost hostile, disagreements between Operations and Sales. This was the cultural and Leadership gap that needed to be, if not solved, at least closed. But, first, I needed to prove my credibility. That is always the first task, whether as a consultant, contractor, or employee. So, I went to work on some early projects to do so. The first was to look at the Cost Structure to see if pricing compared to costs were in synchronization. As with most companies, this was a high mix operation, in this case of the business, there were over 2000 distinct products, so this project took a while. The first step was to identify what the costs were, compared to what they should be. What they were, was largely derived from a bucket called "allocation", which applied the same number to all products, added to material and labor, to apply to pricing.

The fallacy of this argument has been known for many years, to the Activity Based Costing folks, but hadn't been applied hear. And, there were clearly volume modifiers as well; the higher the volume generally, the more costs were spread across units. This seemed obvious but was not embedded in the system. In one case, a low volume product was selling for $14 each, when it cost over $30 to produce it. High volume products could actually be quoted and sold cheaper by sales. The system was changed to incorporate volume and variable allocation percentages, and the system worked better for all. It seemed much of the Sales problem with operations was that their costs were misstated, limiting their ability to sell some products. This change fixed that, along with providing credibility for the new kid on the block.

Then it was on to Operational issues. It turns out Herbie was a huge, 13-acre piece of equipment called, "The Stacker". Its function was to take raw bundles of lumber, cut and sort them into sheets and sizes, based on customer requirements, and "stack" it into sellable bundles. It encompassed 13 different operations and was not keeping up with Production demands. So, the same Equipment Improvement Process, described in the Semiconductor chapter, was employed here. I went out and found the Baseline OEE was 34% and tried to unofficially bin the losses. Then, we formed the EI and SGA teams from the area. Then, we binned the losses which took some time. The data collection criterial and formats was the first team task after training. All we had to start with was some dubious Unplanned Downtime data. Manual observation, much by my manual observation, revealed many of the other losses. This started as just a "what's going on with the equipment" log, which the team would sort out and bin later. After two weeks of data collection, we held a team meeting for a first pass of binning losses. The team was composed of the Production supervisor, the Maintenance manager, Production Operators, Maintenance tech, and myself. We managed to identify Set up time and Idle time as Cycle 1 themes. The Setup time loss was 16 hours a week, and the idle time loss 21 hours a week, or 37 hours, or a 31% loss of OEE. Keep in mind set up time was still a remnant of running big long batches on the tool. Idle time was then sub binned into No work and No operator, which illustrated mostly no operator. Maintenance was of course relieved that none of the losses were "theirs", and asked to be removed from the team, but I said let's wait for the analysis. Turns out no operator was lunches, breaks, shift changes and other absences that weren't adequately covered. So, improvements were introduced to stagger these things, in order to avoid loss. Idle time dropped from 21 hours to 10, and improvement of 9% OEE

Set up time involved starting with Videotaping of setups and mapping the elements. Turns out, there were three correctible issues. First, there was no attempt to start the next product setup, until the first product was finished, when in fact the next product could be started within a short period after the first product started. This required software modifications, which in part, was the second problem. As there were 13 different process, each of which had to be changed with a different product, it was thought to be more convenient to just change them all the same time. In fact, a sequential change could allow the second product to begin sooner. Also, some of the programming changes could be preprogrammed to be planned for the changeover. Maintenance technicians and engineers were key in implementing these changes, answering the "what does this have to do with us" question. Finally, better planning of the wood bundles and unbanding operations prior to running could also save time. These improvements, once implemented reduced set up time from 16 hours to 7, resulting in an 8% OEE improvement. Together with the Idle time improvements, a 17% improvement in OEE was affected, and the constraint significantly improved.

But production continued to ramp, and another cycle was required. Loss binning revealed 21 hours a week in Unplanned and Planned Downtime, an 18% loss of OEE. Sub binning revealed that 9 hours was unplanned downtime and 13 hours was Planned Downtime. First, some fundamental questions needed to be asked, such as how much of the planned downtime was preventing unplanned downtimes. And, how Planned downtime was based on knowledge and experience of the techs, and how much was based on the Equipment Manufacturers specs. How much maintenance was spent on improving the equipment, not just maintaining it. And, finally, were there any routine maintenance tasks that could be performed by operators (Transfer Zone), freeing up maintenance for other work. All these questions were asked and discussed during cycle 2. Fortunately, the head of Maintenance, who initially went along because his boss told him to, became an advocate of the process, and was invaluable to the progress of the team. During the investigation, it turned out there was a part change they had been trying to make for years, that would improve both the performance and speed of the machine. Maintenance had been pushing this for years, but the $100k price tag was considered prohibitive. Luckily, part of my job was to manage the Capital process, and with TPM data and compelling arguments (it was essential for the ramp), the request was approved. Once installed, it paid for itself within three months and improved OEE by 6%. Planned maintenance was changed from time based to unit based, which surprisingly resulted in less PM time. Pilots in Predictive Maintenance, utilizing sensors, saved another 3%. Overall Downtime, Planned and Unplanned, went to eight hours a week, and resulted in an

11% OEE improvement. Another part of this improvement was to take advantage of the 48 hours a week the machine wasn't running, in order to do Maintenance. This was only partially embraced in the past, due to the odd hours it required for Maintenance personal. So, the second cycle yielded 22 additional product hours a week, and an improvement of OEE of 18%. Combined with first cycle improvements, the OEE had moved from the low 30's to the low 60%, and the constraint no longer existed.

So, here we were, with an experienced, motivated team. Do we go to cycle 3, or move to another area, another set of improvements? Fortunately, the business kind of decided for us. By then we were deep into the strategic planning process and had come to an objective to significantly reduce inventory. More on this later, but for now it suggested the Stacker needed to run smaller batch sizes and triple the number of setups they needed to do. So, the third cycle revisited setup, and also chose minor stoppages as themes. Part of the "no good deed shall go unpunished" sub theme, as the original setup reductions enabled the inventory reductions, and now the team had to work on it again. Set up and minor stoppage bins with the new Production plan, with new batch sizes were 21 and five hours, respectively. Remember, we were running weekly, rather than three to six-week batches of product.

So, back to the process.

For setup reduction: Phase three setup reduction.

We implemented Robotic Stackers and Loaders to decrease the time between jobs.

We unbanded all lumber on the loader, rather than when it went into the machine

We provided an early warning signal that a setup change was due shortly, so an operator could preprogram the next job, and make sure everything was ready.

Set up time reduced from 21 hours to 12, a savings of 9 hours a week.

For Minor Stoppages:

We put in line lights and alarms, so stoppages could be cleared sooner.

We took care of over 100 yellow tags to take care of dirt, dust, and grease abnormalities.

We refurbished belts and gears on the tool.

Minor stoppage time reduced from 5 hours to 2, a savings of three hours a week.

These improvements brought the OEE up to 84%, close to the Japanese benchmark, and well over demand OEE of 74%. The Team declared success but continued data monitoring and Initial Clean and Inspection.

A word on Planned Maintenance: In the old days, when the process was just beginning, and called Total Productive Manufacturing. It is called a "TPM Pillar". Here are some elements and some stories.

The place to start with this pillar is to review the "Levels of Maintenance", as follows:

BDM, break down maintenance, the idea of maintaining the machine every time is breaks, Level 1

TBM, time-based maintenance, the idea of doing maintenance is a predetermined elapsing of time, Level 2

UBM, unit-based maintenance, the idea of doing maintenance every certain number of units, Level 3.

AM, Autonomous Maintenance, the idea of operators being trained and certified to do some maintenance tasks, Level 4

CBM, Condition based Maintenance, the idea of doing maintenance when a critical specification gets out of a control limit, Level 5

PDM, Predictive Maintenance: Predictive maintenance evaluates the condition of equipment by performing periodic or continuous (online) equipment condition monitoring. Most predictive maintenance is performed while equipment is operating normally to minimize disruption of everyday operations. Similar to condition-based maintenance, but more sensor based, rather than control charts, Level 6

The goal is to review all tasks and see how high up the scale it is optimal to go. Not all tasks are amenable to higher levels. Even breakdown maintenance is an acceptable strategy in some cases. Another element of the PM pillar is "Spare Parts Control". This is normally a large improvement opportunity for Maintenance, especially in high tech. Some basic Lean principles apply. Label and mark everything and put high usage items as close to the point of use. Adjust replenishment levels to the level of Maintenance being performed. Streamline the paperwork process. If you have "Maintenance Work Orders", find a better way. These are some basics.

So, back to the Tacoma Lumber company:

We then embarked on a Project with Fed Ex to make, package, and ship directly to the customer a product we produced. Previously, product would only to be sent to Home Depot, and customers would purchase it there. So, we worked with Customer Service, IT, FED Ex and Accounting, as a cross functional team to get this accomplished. We set up a special area in the factory to make, package, and label the product, and went to a Fed Ex generated data base to see where to ship it, nationwide. This was a while back, and E commerce was fairly nonexistent then, but the pilot was successful, and Sales of this product substantially increased.

I also traveled to their other four production sites, primarily doing training CANDO and flow work. It was in Eugene, Oregon that I met Nick. He was the Plant manager, had been there 20 years, consistently posted the best numbers of any plant, and hated everything done, and about Corporate. He was a rebel, but untouchable due to his performance. Do you have such a person in your organization?

So, I went to see Nick. I asked the VP of Operations how to handle the situation, and he advised, "just let Nick be Nick". Somehow, I got him to allow me to take a look at the Operation, and do my training event (okay, you can call it a Kaizen). In the class, Supervisors opened up, and said any ideas for improvements had to come from Nick. And, during the event, many improvement ideas from the floor arose. When I went to Nick about the improvements and said most had been considered and dismisses. So, I went home with my tail between my legs, and thought I couldn't make progress here. A month later, I was called into the VP of Operations office, and I was told Nick had implemented many of the improvements that came out of the workshop. I suppose they had to come from him. The VP, by the way and excellent Lean Leader, said, "it doesn't matter who the improvements came from, as long as they were made".

Words of wisdom, and subsequent visits to Eugene, somehow, didn't feel the same.

By now you must be thinking that this lean work is simple and straightforward, form a cross functional team, work on something important, use simple problem-solving tools, and change metrics if needed. And, as I am writing, I'm thinking the same thing. But most implementers mess up on one or more of these things, but they are relatively easy to fix. And, now we get to the complicated part of the Lean triad, the culture change and the Leadership behavior change, and these things get very dicey. At the lumber company in Washington, this had a chance to be positively demonstrated.

The owners were brothers, who were company famous for sitting on the balcony outside their offices, which faced the factory, smoking cigars, and criticizing and laughing at company operations. But these brothers liked what they had seen with Lean in operations and called me in to talk about this "Lean Enterprise" stuff they had read about in a magazine. I told them about culture change and Leadership behavior, and they wanted more details. I was an expert in Lean from an Operations perspective but had limited experience in leading Culture and Leadership changes. For a while it didn't occur to me, then there didn't seem to be willing Leadership partners.

So, I suggested experts in the field, and the owners told me to go find them. After several interviews, I selected Next Level Partners as our initial guides for the process. I asked them to come in and give a presentation to Senior Staff. During the meeting, there were many glazed over eyes and mental shaking of heads, but also much enthusiasm and interest. Next Level Partners are ex Danaher executives, and DBS (Danaher Business System) had a reputation as one of the finest in the world. CFO and the VP of Operations were very interested, the VP of Sales far less so. With the owner's support, we hired them, and the first step was an off-site meeting with the top 30 or so managers and leaders in a three-day Strategic Planning session.

Danaher explains DBS quite simply, "The **Danaher Business System"** (DBS) is the engine at the heart of our success. DBS keeps us ahead of the competition, makes us better operators and creates world-class leaders. It's a set of tools that enables continuous improvement around lean, growth and leadership". Succinct, but right on the money. Danaher is also known for many acquisitions, and the first thing they do is to implement DBS to the acquired company. One of the core parts is "Policy deployment", which is defined as the implementation of a corporate strategy, lack of which plays at least some role in most corporate failures. Therefore, policy deployment is defined as the translation of corporate strategy into action. Workers cannot implement a strategy they do not know. Don't do a Hoshin if you are bad at it, which I was for years. Remember the "Catch ball" piece of it.See a generic example below

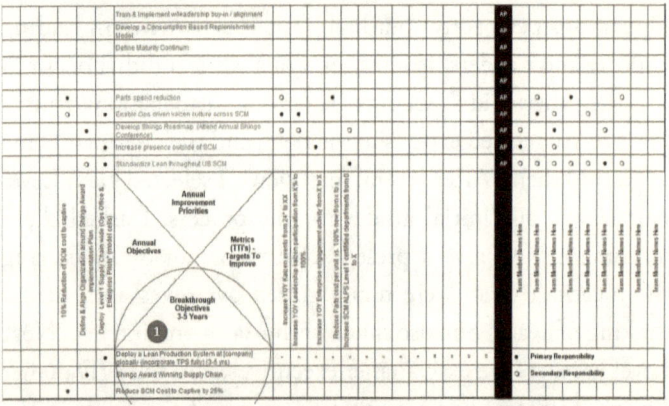

I had done some Hoshin's before, and thought I knew the process, but had never experienced anything like this. The first day was spent training on the system and trying to get consensus and agreement on what the companies' priorities were. This was a new experience, which is usually decided by the VP and owners. As you might expect, there was much disagreement, for which supporting data needed to be provided. Then, the long list of Priorities was ranked based on Impact and Control, a scoring system rather than the prementioned matrix. The results were surprising but agreed to by all. The limit of Strategic Priorities to work on in any given year is three, with two preferred. We then broke into Sub Teams, each cross functional, to determine As-IS and Should Be states and metrics. We kept track of this on a massive spreadsheet, which NLP controlled and was displayed on a large screen, as we were working. The goals were agreed to, then we had to go back again to be "more aggressive" in the goal setting. We did this and reported back. The VP's of the Operation were not permitted on these teams, then they were called in for review.

The next day, we came back for Day 2. It is an interesting group dynamic that everyone comes back to the same seat in a multiday conference. For fun, I changed name tags around to different places, to give the session a more cross functional bent. When people came in, they were "dazed and confused" about where to sit. An interesting social experiment. NLP comprised all the work we had done in Teams and put it into the SPM (Strategic Planning Matrix). We then sanity checked the matrix to see if we had the resources and money to support the process. Fewer is better, warning us of the amount of work and resources required was the mantra. We chose three, one on cash, one on people improvements, one on Sales processes. Operations was oddly missing from the list but would have to be heavily involved in other process, and the previous Lean work in Operations would continue. These were all broken down into project plans, teams and general timelines. One of the unique parts of the process was to have a Team sponsor be from outside the area being worked on. For example, the CFO oversaw the Ops improvement team. A lean team was also deployed to implement the process, and they needed a leader. Everybody's head turned toward me, and I tried to look away. But I was appointed Lean Leader, and appointed a team of three, a Customer Service person, a Finance Person, and myself. I was the only team member who knew anything about lean, so I spent the first week training the team, as well as interested others.

Then, we got to work on the first objective, priority one, which was to improve cash flow. As inventory, especially Finished Goods, had a high inventory carrying cost, we were tasked to work on that. A strategic objective was to make the company more "loan worthy", so it could invest in needed capital. Ratios such as Inventory turnover rate and Days of Carry were not looking good and deteriorating. It certainly helped that the Stacker improvements had enabled Operations to reduce cycle time from three weeks to about three days. So, in Lean terminology, replenishment times had been significantly reduced. But Sales had a different idea, which was "we don't ever want to run out of anything, ever," and cited rare but actual events of emergency weather related pole replacements to prove their case. They were also skeptical that Operations had reduced the cycle time that much, and pointed out low volume, highly variable products as exceptions that negated the rule.

Time to get everyone together and work this out. So, a cross functional team was formed to develop a system to save inventory carrying cost, and at the same time, keep customer service levels high. I don't know if you want to call it a Kaizen, but it certainly wasn't an "event". Six weeks of grind it out, get the concerns and details on the table, and lots of discussion led to the countermeasure. With IT's help, a replenishment system was defined where a trigger was sent to production when FG levels reached replenishment levels, with rather healthy safety stocks. This worked for 80% of the products, and the 20% of Low Volume, highly erratic products remained on the old system. FG inventories reduced by more than half, and cash was freed up.

Most importantly, relationships were built between Operations and Salespeople that had not been formed before. This became the start of the Culture change in the company.

On to objective 2, why was HR selected as a key Policy Deployment goal? It spoke to the culture of the company regarding Management/Employee relations and the role of HR in the business. The long time VP of HR had left under uncertain conditions, and the department was being run by an inexperienced manager.

I can't emphasize enough how important a Policy Deployment is to the success of Lean. In the words of State Farm Insurance, "Don't Leave Home without it" So, on to people. This broke down into the following areas:

Current Employee Involvement and Support

We started with the simple question of "What is the role of HR"? The consensus response was "to avoid litigation for the company". It didn't seem to be an inspiring or motivating role for the department. But this is what they believed. The inquiry began with "who is the customer", and it turned out not to be the employees. This was illustrated by the payroll process, which required several hours of manual entry to an outdated system each day and week by Supervisors. This was done to "ensure integrity of the process". Meetings involving IT revealed there was an easy fix to provide an exception-based reporting system, which saved supervisors four to six hours a week of mindless data entry and reduced errors. The new system was implemented within three months, allowing supervisors to be on the floor, where they belonged, and reducing errors.

Hiring and Retention

The cases of myself and the VP of HR were used for pilots to analyze the current system and recommend improvements. Firstly, hiring requirements were vaguely put, and not clearly defined, e.g. what did the company want from me, and why did it take six months to figure it out. Also, hiring decisions were largely made by hiring department managers, with little or no input of departments that would have huge impact on the new hires job. After much discussion, and some heated disagreement, it was decided to go to a cross functional hiring panel to decide on new hires. We used the Lean/Industrial Engineering position for my Lean team, who basically replaced me, as a pilot for this process. We gathered the panel, trained them on recruitment methods and procedures, and brought in candidates to be interviewed by the panel. Two candidates for my Lean Engineer position were qualified and good hires. The panel decided on a person, where I, as the hiring manager, would have picked another one, but I had to live with the decision of the process. It turned out to be a good decision, better than the one I could have made myself. Spreading this to the Sales positions turned out to be another problem but was eventually adopted and even the VP of HR position was filled by panel. We needed to help the panels with sample questionnaires, training on interviewing, and careful selection of the panel, but the talent acquired appeared to be better organizational fits.

HR Roles and Responsibilities.

This was primarily teaching HR about who is the customer, and it being the employees, as well as the litigation prevention role they had primarily taken on. Countermeasures included HR to employee training, improved communication on changes and corporate doings, listening to employee ideas on changes to long standing policies and the like. I really didn't like the "Employee Satisfaction survey", but employees seemed happy to be involved. HR also periodically participated in morning huddles, which were eye openers for them. They previously rarely left their offices.

IT

The Information Technology department was hugely helpful in developing the Sharepoint app.

This included E mail notifications to RED tasks for appropriate team members, Sharing of the app to the right people, Leadership Summaries, and the rest. Then, it was time to look into their Internal operations. This project was about how work was done internally vs. contracted, much of it was contracted, with iffy verification and validation of vendors. Much of this was around Sales Links to Salespeople, commissions and the like, and support of current systems. A review of this led to $80k a year in reduction of contract cost, with no additional IT staffing.

Lean Warehouse:

The company had a large warehouse which had a variety of purchased material and WIP from internal process. I was asked to look at it for improvements. The first thing was to rearrange materials based on pull usage and volume. This meant relocation in terms of vertical and horizonal space. It also meant reviewing and dealing with inventory that hasn't been used for years. We also improved "Pull lists" to be location based and repaired and improved pallets and material handling equipment. Also, labeling and Marking the shelfs with product ID and Bar Code scanning codes, for easier and quicker transaction processing. The Warehouse Supervisor, Josh and employee input, some of whom suggested they had been suggesting these things for years.

So, the company, now financially stable, and with a bunch of cash for the owners, who retired. The new owners were not so hot for this "Lean stuff", and with most of the Senior Leadership staff, chose to move on. I was joined in the "defection" from several other senior management people who became enamored with Lean and couldn't go back to an environment without it.

So, for me time to move on again, seeming like some kind of job hopper, when external circumstances determined my fate. So, no I wound up in a different place, upstate New York, and a different industry, Medical Equipment, the one described in the opening section of the book.

This was the worst Lean experience of my life, both professionally and personally. So, what went wrong? After three years and over $3 million of investment, costs were up, and quality was down. What did I see in my six-week experience with this company? First, Strategic Plan, if you want to call it that, was to follow the consultants, who I had previous negative experience with. Probably an unfair bias. But their philosophy was if you could make a single piece as fast as possible, you could make many parts faster. There are many issues with this approach, but volume production is just basically different than small lot size production. And, your company is not necessarily "high mix, low volume", if 90% of your processes are common.

So, the strategy was to take one large assembly line, and convert them into Product Specific "One Piece Flow lines", making an individual product, one piece at a time. The approach was validated by data showing the first piece off a line came much faster, although orders were filled at a slower rate than before, and synchronizing production off these lines was an impossible task. When I showed up, 13 of these lines were in place, with a plan for the rest. And, all the effort was devoted to Final Assembly, when there were clearly issues with upstream processes.

The second problem was the conversion strategy. Each of the previous 13 were done via fiveday Kaizen's, with the usual recipe. Day 1 Lean training, mostly a sales pitch for the approach, Day 2 organizing for the change, Day 3 going to the line for the conversion, Day 4, running pilots and preparing for the Management presentation, and Day 5, the Management presentation. The Management had no choice but to wildly applaud the team's effort, never questioning the approach or whether it was the right problem. This is one of the first Lean Leadership question, "Are we working on the right thing". Not done here.

So, I attended the 14th version of this. Well scripted, well taught, and executed to a T, per script, with zero acknowledgement to special line needs or product differences. I found it horrible, and although I participated, I was roundly criticized by Management and the Lean people, for not being a "Team Player". Oh, well.

The next problem was the approach to Gemba Walks and Huddles. The approach was unique, and to me, weird, basically doing this were helpful in this process without going to the line. It was done in the morning, in a hallway, with the metrics displayed on a display board. No one came within 500 feet of the line, and no one asked any process questions, it was a show for Management to show they were participating. No practical use whatsoever. When questioning the consultants about this spouted some non-sense about it being a cleanroom environment (it wasn't) and getting some way of getting leadership involved.

They were also teaching "Leadership Standard Work", which is a good concept, but hard to implement. They would have each manager and up fill out paperwork describing their daily work, and fitting into a schedule, then see if it was being followed. It didn't seem to matter much what the work was, as long as it was standardized. Having been an operational leader for a long time, I recognized the Leadership was, most days, organized chaos, and couldn't be scripted. The important thing was to get to the line, ask process questions, let go of decisions where possible, and ensure problems were getting resolved.

So, after the first three weeks, I was discouraged, and reported to the VP my findings, as described above. He listened carefully, emphasized with my approach, and then shared he was quitting in two weeks. He advised me to focus on other areas in my remaining time, it was a sixmonth contract, and try to show a new approach in other areas. So, I started projects in a feeder line, and in Molding, using the TPM approach as an entry point described above. I also taught the Supply Management people PFOP, Policy for Every Part, as inventory was totally out of control, and turned less than two times. We made some progress, but the new Leadership, who was basically the old Leadership, didn't appreciate my comments or efforts, and terminated my contract. Two years later, 30%o of the workforce was laid off, and the companies Lean efforts suspended.

Lessons Learned for this Experience

1. Don't attempt to save a sinking ship that doesn't want to be saved.

2. Don't try to improve things if Leadership is not committed to the change

3. One-piece flow is a nice concept, but often not applicable. Process commonality and learning to mix model sequence is more important.

4. Start with real strategic planning and be sure you are working on the right things.

5. Dictate the strategy to the consultant not the other way around.

So. Cal High Tech

So, again, time to move on. I was contracted for three months with a company in Southern California, who used to make cell phones, but now was more into high tech electronics. They had an "America" after their name but were clearly a Japanese company. My three-week assessment provided little disagreement from Management in the meeting, so I went forward.

Most of the initial projects were Manufacturing related, all though I did get into some Finance stuff later. Despite the "America" after their name, the company was still largely and in detail directed from Japan. Each area had a Japanese "advisor" in the office, and the daily "calisthenics" were still performed in all areas. The president, who I became close to, was clearly a figurehead, whose goal was not to lead, but to follow instruction.

Two of the areas, perceived as constraints to customer delivery, were in the San Diego plant, with the third being in the Juarez, Mexico twin plant. All the areas were Cleanrooms, similar to Semiconductor, and amenable to the wafer process described above. One difference was the constraint was hard to identify in one area, and the inventory so small in size that it could not be easily identified. So, the pull system was implemented, and the counting of cards became a reliable method of determining the constraint for TPM, as well as for manning. Another issue was some of the inspection machines, which were requiring 100% inspections, although there were few failures. The machine inspection was then validated by a manual inspection. Too much inspection sounds like blasphemy, but in this case turned out to be true. Sampling proved to be an effective and correcting some small machine issues eliminated the need for manual inspection.

The twin plant operation that was the constraint was largely fixed by pull, flow and simple operational tool improvements. The constraint was lifted, and operations improved.

A word now about Leadership. The company was big on "Communication". This meant weekly gatherings, where the company president would share results and news. It was done monthly in Juarez. Attendance was compulsory. A good idea, but little or nothing was shared about process, employee line issues or countermeasures. The idea was to share information, rather than help. I didn't push Leadership on this but should have.

Naming the program seemed to be an important piece. As with many companies, various CI efforts had been tried before, with little or limited success. So, a naming protocol was important. It was decided to name it, "Lean 4.0", as three other attempts over the years had "failed". So, banners were made and posted, and something was supposed to be different. It has been long and widely discussed the difference in culture between Japanese and Western culture when it comes to Lean, but it's largely true. Trying to splice American Lean into a

Japanese company, regardless of its location, is a difficult and trying exercise, one that I'm not sure has ever been solved.

So, now to the Finance example. We were again, struggling to the "Overhead Absorption" question. Some processes, especially high-tech ones, had extra costs as compared to "Mature Businesses", whatever that means. But costs were allocated across the board as "Site Manufacturing Costs" and sent up the Finance Food chain to product and site profitability cost.

This is a dangerous and potentially fatal exercise, but one still practiced by many companies. I offered to lead a team focused on this but was turned down from Japan.

So, having made progress on my initial projects, and trying to decide what to do next, I was offered an extension of my contract, but had to decline due to the cultural and Leadership issues. As least I recognized this by knowing. So, where to go and what to do? So, what do to now? Good luck to the Company, maybe Lean 5.0 will work.

I was interested in the Toyota Production process and was intrigued by another Southern California High tech company interested in implementing Lean. I was further intrigued by the fact that the VP of Operations, and the VP of Quality were ex Toyota people, who had learned TPS at the detail level, and thought I could learn something. Instead, I learned different lessons. So, I went to work at a Fabrication facility in Southern California. The first year, I was assigned to Fab 1, a high-tech screen-printing operation, kind of like making miniature T Shirts. which was more amenable to Lean? After implementing pull, Visual Controls, morning meetings, and other Lean tools, we ran into the FDA, for a set of machine changes needed for a hearing aid product. We worked through this issue and developed enhanced maintenance and operational procedure to support the FDA requirement. Pilots and testing took a while, although the changes to the machines were quite small. Welcome to the world of regulation. We faced other issues as well. One was running into my old favorite the MRP system, which the corporate bosses insisted we use. We started running out of materials at a rapid rate, and my study indicated pull from a Kanban would be more reliable for 80% of the products. Of course, the proposal was turned down by corporate.

So, then Management decided I should work in Fab 2, a higher tech, and higher business impact than Fab 1. The problem was the culture of the Fab 2 culture was a highly Engineering controlled process set of parameters. Orders got further and further behind, and process issues were perceived as all legitimate process Engineering issues. There was no Continuous improvement work, because all process was perfect, and didn't need help. So, I assigned to Fab 1 which was much more amenable to Lean and had much more willing Leadership. A favorable environment usually yields positive results, and we had that in Fab 1. Improvements were made in printers, assembly, communication and problem solving. Part of this was resisting the recipe driven Toyota approach, which was difficult. Given the corporate VP experience, another interesting side bar was to appeal to the FDA for a hearing aid product that had to made. We needed to make Equipment improvements to accede to these requests, and they required us to make the changes. The FDA has facetious requirements to make a product change, which were challenging, and in our view, unnecessary but we made them and moved on. Also, the ex-Toyota VP of Ops came, and gave us suggestions about layout changes, and other "lean" things he thought important. The changes didn't make sense to the Fab manager or me, and with the help of the VP of Quality and the Plant Manager, managed to avoid making these changes.

The second year, given quite impressive results in Fab 1, I was moved to Fab 2, and warned by Senior Management that it would be much more challenging than Fab 1. And so, it was. I started with Electronic Testing of a Genesis product, for a key customer on a tester we had no experience with, and no Test Engineers. It was the Fab constraint, as product was delayed to our Aerospace customer. We had previously subcontracted this outside, but Senior Management decided that was too costly, and we could do it internally. We had never done Electronic testing before, so this became quite a challenge. We didn't know what we were doing, mis installed the software, and would up with yields in the 20% range. The company asked me to help, I suppose I knew as much about Electronic testing as anyone else. My boss, the VP of Quality and I developed a simple data base that would track rejects and causes to try and get a handle on what was happening. Reinstallation of the software, tracing of issues to upstream processes, (Lam Etchers) and fixing vendor problems with tape (Dupont) brought Yield up to the high 60's. It was basically an Equipment Improvement cycle and got us out of trouble. Operator training, further defect analysis and learning curve brought the yield to the mid to high 80's, and our critical Aerospace customer got off our backs.

Then, the next constraint came up. You know, it's like that in Manufacturing; fix A, and B comes up, until you are on ZZ before you know it. Therefore, a deep understanding of Problem Solving is so critical. This constraint was Plating yield, from a nearby outside vendor. The testing fix had given me a modicum of respectability of with Fab 2 Engineers, but I needed some more. I got assigned full time to the vendor to "fix the plating issues". Technically, I was about as much an expert on Plating, as I was on Electrical Testing. But, in this work, one becomes a fast learner and a versatile resource to the organization. So, deeply I dove into Plating. Many things were discovered and fixed. Type and amounts of chemical dips, operations procedures, carriers, lot sizes, and inspections were all addressed. The yield improved from the high 40%'s to the high 80%'s, again in the magic 13-week cycle, and my credibility was further established. But what if I don't have thirteen weeks is a commonly asked question. Well, containment actions can be put in place, but if the root causes are not addressed, the problem is likely to return, and your company will have to fix it many times. So, better to get to root cause and preventative countermeasures, no matter how long and painful it may appear. This is one of the most important Lean lessons to learn.

So, the next major issues that came up in Thin Film was an area called Fill and Debridge. The mostly automated process had one place where manual labor was still prevalent. The product had to soldered and inspected after soldering. There were 16 operators in the area, and they were working 10-hour days, 6 days a week, trying to keep up with demand. Remember the Lean lesson about getting the problem right. The perceived issues were poor operator workmanship, bad supervision, and poor planning. Nothing about the process could possibly be wrong, according to the Engineering staff. Another key Lean lesson that cannot be stressed enough: get the problem right.

Top leadership's solution was to hold a Kaizen event, a strange request for a constraint operation that was already behind schedule. A strange request, especially from ex Toyota people; as you know, the next Kaizen event Toyota holds will be it's first. So, corporate said to do it, so I gathered 20 people, including 16 operators, into a room, and started the training. To my surprise and joy, after 45 minutes the Plant Manager walked into the room and ordered the people back to work.

Bless his heart! He told me to keep this between us and asked me to go fix the problem.

So, I spent the next three days observing, timing, talking to the operators and taking notes on the process steps and variance. Call it an informal Value Stream Map if you wish, but I was just trying to figure it out. It didn't really take that long. The operators were spending 80%of their time fixing Solder Machine defects, and no one had ever asked the question, "Why does the Solder Machine create so many defects". Engineering pushed back, insisting this was a complicated product, and the soldering was a perfect process. So, I investigated what the key parameters were to make a good solder joint. Again, I knew as little about as I did about plating or electronic testing, but I was a quick learner, and an experienced problem solver. Which, people, is often what you need.

Soldering was about having the belt in good condition, having the soldering zones all at the right temperature, a having the distance between products being correct, and a few other controllable factors. We fixed the small niches in the belt, controlled all the soldering zone temperatures, set a standard for distance between products, and a few other minor changes. I could hear the laughter from Engineering, from the protection of their offices. So, after spending $1400 on machine improvements, which was incredibly hard to get approved, and careful presentation of the data, I was "allowed" to run a 20-piece trial.

Before we discuss the result, let's look at the impact on the operators. They were working 58 hours weeks, looking at bad microscopes and magnifying glasses to pick out tiny soldering defects. Then, picking out the tiny defects with tweezers. The tools for this were abysmal, and I immediately got better tools for the operators., despite budgetary constraints. They were grateful and appreciative, but it didn't solve the true problem.

So, back to the 20-piece run. Eighteen pieces were perfect, and the other two had minor defects. Previously, almost every piece had to be reworked. I called the Engineers out, along with Top management, and I couldn't tell whether the look was chagrin, surprise, or astonishment. So, they had no choice but to accept the changes, and within a short time, the schedule was on time, and the constraint broken.

I was happy about this, but even more pleased by the reaction of the operators. Make the work easier for the operators, is a long standing, but important Lean concept. Not only was the overtime work ended, but staffing was reduced in half, with operators being redeployed to other areas, and certainly more pleasant work. A very satisfying experience in my career, with a variety of learning lessons.

So, on to the next problem, which was a three million-dollar HTCC machine. It wasn't keeping up with Production demands. So, it became my project to investigate it. In this organization, Equipment Improvement Teams weren't doable, so I kind of became my own team. The OEE was 42%, (isn't it always?), and the biggest losses were Planned Downtime and Slow Speed.

Planned Downtime was about changing needles, which was based on a time-based maintenance schedule, and not synchronized so that needles could be changed together. Slow speed, and you may be familiar with the problem, was a result of slowing down the machine to avoid quality problems. The link between speed and defects was somewhat abstract but felt real to Engineering to Management. For Planned Maintenance, changing needle changes to Unit Based, synchronizing changes, so that more were done together, and improved training delivered to the Maintenance techs, cut this loss in half. For Slow Speed, a speed loss of up to 5% a week, and collection of quality loss and downtime date, was done. Turns out, defects didn't increase much when the speed was increased, but was better correlated to machine stops and starts. Good to know.

So, then I left, as my position was being consolidated with a CI guy at corporate. I suppose, in retrospect, I made too many enemies in the company, Engineers generally hate being upstaged, and it was definitely an Engineering driven company.

I also ran the Safety team, which is another lesson. This common thing of 6S, with the 6th S being Safety is at best, absurd, and at worst dangerous. What it has in common with Lean, is identifying and correcting problems.

Lessons Learned Described from this Experience.

Most are described in the narrative, but here is the summary.

1. Get to the root cause and preventative countermeasures. A3 is an excellent tool
2. Make sure you have the problem right. Fixing the wrong problem is one of the most common Lean mistakes.
3. Make the work easier for the Operators
4. Prove credibility for Lean and yourself early in an implementation.
5. Know the true meaning and spirit of Kaizen.
6. Don't mix 5S and Safety
7. Be bold, defy conventional wisdom, don't be afraid to take chances
8. Problem solving ability is as important as technical expertise.

Summary of the experiences:

So, if you've made it this far in this narrative, what can you take with you as far as lessons learned from my 30 years and numerous implantation experiences. Here is a summary of do's and don'ts:

My process always included a three week "Assessment Process". Over the years, I think I have learned to simplify the questions to a critical few. Most importantly, the two main questions are "how do you identify problems", and "once identified, what do you do about it". These are the critical elements of Lean, and as we learn more, we realize this to a greater extent. And what about culture?

> A simple definition:
> Company culture refers to the personality of a company. It defines the environment in which employees work. Company culture includes a variety of elements, including work environment, company mission, value, ethics, expectations, and goals.

> And another definition:
> According to Robert E. Quinn and Kim S. Cameron at the University of Michigan at Ann Arbor, there are four types of organizational culture: Clan, Adhocracy, Market, and Hierarchy. Clan oriented cultures are family-like, with a focus on mentoring, nurturing, and "doing things together." See Appendix.

What does this mean for Lean? What questions does it bring up? Is Lean harder to implement in Union environments.

How does Lean affect these cultural elements…Let's take a look.

Clan: Most companies I have worked in have established, informal, "good old boy networks", which can manifest in many ways, departmental, organizationally and others. These networks must be changed to a "lean network", filled with people committed to open discussion, willingness to identify and resolve problems, and create environment where problem solving is a value, rather than an issue. It is a long-standing Lean principle to "Create a favorable environment". This is part of this process.

Adhocracy: The opposite of which is bureaucracy. The Lean question is how to reduce bureaucracy for change. An example of this is the Engineering change process. How many signatures are required to approve and Engineering change? How can this process be simplified? Take a look. Critical process changes that effect customers need to be carefully analyzed, but many are not, and distinctions need to be made. Reduce bureaucracy wherever possible.

Hierarchy: This refers to where decisions are made. Lean argues that decisions are best made at the "point of the process", where the process experts are. Traditional thinking argues that decisions need to be made by the executives in the office, who have little idea what is going on in the line. Establish a firm decision-making process, where decisions are pushed down to the lowest level possible These are interesting and fascinating discussions. Involve a facilitator, expert in meeting and organizational dynamics, in these discussions.

Market

One common statement heard for years is "the customer is always right". No, they are not.

Should Rubbermaid have agreed to make a poor-quality product, so Wal Mart would buy it? Make a high-quality product at the same low cost and figure out how to do it. In Semiconductor, poor yield products would be accepted to "fill the line".

Look closely at internal, as well as external customers. They both matter. Send the next process a high quality, reliable product they don't have to send back.

Simplify all of this:

Lean culture is simply, encouraging identification of problems and getting them solved at the "lowest" level possible. It's working together in teams, rather than organizational siloes. It's measuring the right things and having a process to do something when the measures are off. It is doing a few amount of key strategic things, and providing these things resources. It is about being humble and trusting your people to do the right thing. Lean culture is about identifying influencers, who may not have been identified before, regardless of position or organizational level

As importantly is what Lean culture is not. Lean culture is not about reducing cost. It is not a program of the month. It is not even, really about eliminating waste. And, it is definitely not about Leadership doing the same things, the same way and expecting to see a difference. It is not about "fixing" Manufacturing and leaving the rest of the business alone.

Advanced Lean Methods:

Do the basics, then move on to this stuff. Hopefully, if you ignore the imported formulas and calculations, this can give you a simple and useful way to get started.

CHAPTER SIX
HOW TO DO A PULL SYSTEM

Basic definitions apply. A Kanban size is (Daily Demand x Replenishment time x Safety factor)/ Package Size. Resist the urge to complicate the simple formula. Adjust as needed as you observe how the process works. Try to reduce the variation via problem solving, and try to reduce the lead times, in order to work Kanban sizes down. It is a little-known fact, once again, that the purpose of Pull and Kanban is to raise and resolve problems.

Let us imagine a downstream process that uses 100 tapes/day (on average).

The lead time to obtain new tapes once the signaled start from the Point of Use (POU), arrive to the upstream (or supplier) and the tapes are delivered to the POU is 5 days. The Safety Stock in percentage is 20% (to compensate demand variation or delays) Every container is of 50 tapes.

Second definition is process disconnect between internal process and Kanban, in order to buffer the process disconnects. This is the process used in Fab photolithography.

Pull can be effective for Supply parts, as well as Work in process parts. Pull does a better job than MRP based systems in replenishing supplies for Purchased Parts.

Keep in mind that Pull applies to repetitive parts, which not every part falls into. Do PFEP (Policy for Every Part) first and see what percentage of parts are "Kanban able". It is usually in the 80-85% range. Use other simple techniques for other parts.

Before we get started on the details, let's dispel some mistaken notions about Repetitive and Pull. It is a common MRP notion that Kanban is just another name for Min/Max in the MRP system. This is a strange and distorted notice, but common among MRP/ERP fanatics. Secondly, the idea of Kanban and Pull is to reduce inventory. It is not. What it is, primarily, is to point out process problems and imbalances (a perfect Lean system has no Kanban's), and secondly to ensure no work is produced before it is needed. So, please understand this, and now, let's dive into the mechanics.

Kanban has many elements:

Kanban Size- This is defined a usage (Daily Demand) x Replenishment time in days x Safety stock percentage/ Package size. Modify the time base on the formula to whatever suits your need (minutes, hours, months, etc.)

Number of Kanban: This is how many packages are needed in the process to meet the demand.

Kanban Form/Type: There are squares, boards, cards and a variety of ways to convey information to an upstream process. Watermarking is an effective method for small parts. Set a level with a piece of tape, and once the level is reached, replenish the bin. Simple and effective.

Kanban Control and Data base. A Data base is normally maintained which keeps track of area Kanbans in the process. If Demand changes, a new number is put in, and Kanban sizes are automatically updated for potential action. Ideally, this is linked to Customer Demand.

Floating Kanban: Special Kanban, used at the discretion of Leadership, to control unexpected variation in demand, mix or supply. Use at your own risk!

Let's use a real-life example of a Pull System in action.

A fabrication facility used Kanban Squares to control the Photo Lithography process, which were four cells of Coat/ Align/ Develop Equipment, plus a subsequent Inspection process. Cards from Implant, Diffusion or Etch (depending on the flow) would come in to Photo attached to the Lot. Sample Kanban Card below.

The lot would go on a shelf, and the card would go on a board, in FIFO order on the board, with hooks. It took us some time to figure out how to control FiFO on a free-standing board. Attachment below. We basically used a set of directional arrows indicating what space was first, and what the flow are cards was. Lots that came in would go to the first space to the right of the Start hook, unless Supervision needed to change the order. Processing into the next coater would be the first card to the right of the hook. Cards would be reattached to the lot box when the job went back into the process.

Between Coat and Photo, there would be a square that would allow two lots, usually including the one being processed. Two lots were allowed because Photo processing time was longer than coat time.

Between Coat and Develop, there was a Kanban square= 1 lot, as develop was a faster process than Photo. There was a Kanban square of four lots between Develop and Inspection.

When completed, lots would go forward to the next process, based on Traveler and Kanban Card information, and cards would go back to the previous process. This is an important point, Lots forward, cards back.

A similar system with cards and squares was deployed in other Fab areas. Starts were controlled when initial diffusion steps were completed. Temporary Kanban cards were strategically deployed during Long Downtime events or other extraordinary occurrences. These exceptions had to be approved by the Fab Manager and causes and countermeasure were tracked. Identified Constraints had larger Safety Factors applied.

A data base, with modified demand was run every other week, and changes to the pull system notifications were sent to Fab Supervisors. At first, the system was considered cumbersome and unwieldy, but after a while was embraced as an effective tool.

How to misuse Kanban systems:

In a lumber company, we had a medium volume Sawn product that required raw material. We have most items in the Warehouse on Pull, including this item. Unbeknownst to me and my team, the Sales VP had gone to China, and negotiated a great price, the only way the product could be delivered is by a full shipload, which was a two plus year supply. We had no space in the Warehouse for the boatload, and I was instructed to find a place to put this stuff. It was a classic right solution to the wrong problem. Increasing the package size to "1 Shipload" seemed unreasonable. And soon, the second shipload was due to leave China. So, after vigorous debate, we decided to find a state wide supplier, whose cost was about 20% higher, but whose total cost was actually less. This supplier delivered every two weeks, and product quality was actually higher. Plus, a product Engineering change came along, which would have scrapped all Chinese inventory.

Remember, always pull, for the replenishable parts. Use PFEP (policy for every part) to sort that out. Be careful about frequent changes to Usage or Replenishment times. Change safety factors instead. Don't ever allow more physical space for parts than the Kanban size. They will get overfilled. Get smaller bins or block off physical spaces instead. Don't ever lose a Kanban card. Conduct card counts periodically. Card number on the bottom indicates the total number of cards for that part. I have found Kanban cards in the strangest places, desk drawers, lab coats, trash cans, just about everywhere. Remember, "no tickee, no washee", e.g. no card, no replenishment.

Hopefully, by the time you are reading this book, the 2020 crises we are facing is well behind us. There is a pull lesson in Toilet Paper, however. Before the crisis hit, we, being a Lean family had one roll of toilet paper on the rack, and one under the bathroom sink. Then, because of Package size changes, the replenishment size was increased to four. Then, rather suddenly, supply disappeared overnight. Plus, "Usage" increased because everyone was staying at home. So, what to do. For us, we increased Safety Factor to one package, and added one temporary Kanban to the mix, in case something appeared. We did not change Usage or Replenishment Time.

CHAPTER SEVEN
LINEARITY, HEJUNKA, AND MIXED MODEL SEQUENCING

These topics all fall under the topic of level loading. In level 1, linearity to the daily rate is measured as follows: Let's explain: This topic is about "make the daily rate every day", measure the absolute deviations to the daily rate., trace cause to daily rate deviations. Too much Production is as much of an absolute deviation as too little production. More complex is "make the daily mix every day", a very complex problem to solve. This is far different from my experience of "make the month", where there would be much scrambling, angst and overtime spent the last few days of the month, to "make the numbers". This would clean out the line and create a self-fulfilling prophecy for the next month. This is a key Lean cultural change, and a difficult one to implement. Train Leadership on the concept and implications, and hope they listen.

Linearity is defined by the daily rate minus the sum of the deviations, divided by the daily rate.

Drive this up first, to the 85% to 90% range, otherwise Mixed Model Sequencing is likely to fail.

Or, if the daily rate was 100 units, and 90 were produced, the calculation with be the daily rate, 100, minus the deviation (100-90), divided by the daily rate, 100, or 90%. And of course, if you make 110, with a schedule of 100, the deviation is the same. "Overproduction is as bad as underproduction" is a hard pill to swallow, but a key operational and cultural change, if you can manage it. What do you do if operators finish the daily rate in 6 hours? Have team or quality circle meetings, do extra clean and inspection; analyze linearity deviations and countermeasures. Go work in other areas. Try as best you can to avoid putting "hay in the barn"

And, critically, what was the cause of the deviation? Keep track of this over a month or so and see if you can see problems to be resolved.

Please carefully study mixed model sequencing for common processes before going off "halfcocked" on one-piece flow or dedicated product lines. Even product lines with some diversity can be handled in Lean with "Feeder lines" into the main process. This is an advanced Lean concept, and not for the faint of heart.

Most of your lines are probably more complex than the "two door, four door" examples given in much of the literature. This is a problem smart Lean engineers can figure out. Almost all of the literature and wisdom on this is for automotive options, which is probably not your business.

The general formula is listed but means little without discussion and product understanding. To be honest, I've never used the formulas, just figured it out with my team.

- TT: Takt time of the entire line (the line takt)
- TTn: Takt time for product n
- Pn: Percentage of the produced items that are of type n

Then the general formulas would be as follows:

$$TT = \sum_{n=1}^{k} TT_n \cdot P_n$$

$$\sum_{n=1}^{k} P_n = 100\%$$

Don't worry about the formulas and the calculations. The above is just for you formula freaks. Work on making the daily rate every day and analyzing deviation causes. That brings huge benefits and culture change.

A few words about Takt time. Most of you know the term and it is asked in almost every Lean job interview. And, it is fundamentally meaningless. Of course, we know it is "drumbeat production", or one every xxx, and it should match customer demand. Nice concept, but rarely used in my experience. There are many drums beating at once, and volume, mix, and material changes almost every instant. Trying to set a line to Takt time is a daunting task. Make the daily rate every day, drive that to 85%, try your hand at Mixed Model sequencing, then call me about Takt time. In summary, running to Takt time is a nice philosophical concept, but not really practical in todays world.

How to do Mixed Model Sequencing, MMS

Mixed Model Sequencing is an advanced Lean technique, that should be used if appropriate and applicable. A primer. Be sure to get the pull system running smoothly first. Do not attempt MMS from MRP or a schedule. Rely only on the pull system, and what is being signaled from the downstream process. Also, be sure that setup times have been reduced, as MMS will not work without low setup times. So, in simple language, if there are multiple products with a similar process, the question becomes how to mix the product starts into the line. So. A simple example:

The Pull system indicates there are twice as many pulls from Product A as Product B. The setup time to convert from A to B is 8 minutes, as Set up time was addressed with the

Equipment Improvement process. So, how to run the line. First of all, adjust Kanban's to adjust the pull for the MMS. Account for the setup time in order to figure it out. So, you may to make two hours of product B, then convert to Product A to facilitate upstream flow. Then, go back to A, and run Product A for four hours, and change again. Balancing setup and run time, and keep in mind the impact on the downstream process. If they are going to Batch produce anyway, no need for you to Mix Model Sequence. Adjust and manage based on the pull system. For high mix, low volume applications, just change once a day, and make the daily rate every day. Don't get too enamored or involved in the formulas. Just fill Kanbans from cards or squares. Let the process be your guide. If process times are too different, consider setting up feeder lines, to support the multiple processes. Always be guided by principles, which in this case, is what best facilitates flow. Discuss with team members on the line.

Introduction:

Mixed Model Production is the practice of assembling several distinct models of a product on the same assembly line without changeovers and then sequencing those models in a way that smoothes the demand for upstream components. The objective is to smooth demand on upstream workcenters, manufacturing cells or suppliers and thereby reduce inventory, eliminate changeovers, improve kanban operation. It also eliminates difficult assembly line changeovers, but remember to work on the changeovers, as part of the TPM process first. Don't put the cart before the horse.

For now, let's abandon the formulas and describe a simple example, and a real-life example in the Windows and Doors business. Let's say there are three products, a Green, Yellow and Red product what share process characteristics other than color. Demand for Green is twice as much as Yellow, which is three times as much as Red. So, let's think about this before applying formulas. What is the downstream changeover time from one product to the next? What is the packaging sized of the various products? Is there any advantage to making these products multiple times a day? Practitioners often want to show off their technical knowledge and formulas without considering business issues. In the above example, making 60 reds, 30 Yellows and 10 Reds was just fine. If you are doing pull, adjust Kanban sizes accordingly. If there is an advantage to multiple run, try a mix of 30, 10 and 5, and see how the system adjusts. Continue reducing until and optimal level is reached, which of course would be 3, 2, 1, ten times a day. Don't go there unless you can and need to. Find an optimal balance.

In the Window and Door example, I was trying to get capacity onto the SGA line from other overloaded lines. At first, I thought this would be simple, as Glazing process were largely the same. I learned a few things from this. First, there were processes before glazing, mostly shaping metal, that were quite specific to a product that were not the same on other lines. For example, welding of a Projected Window was quite different than welding a Sliding Glass Door. Secondly, there was a significant amount of "Tribal Knowledge": information known by specific people that had not been transferred to others. This was made more critical by having an incomplete Specification system, that did not contain specific details. So, the countermeasures:

1. Improve the specification system with better details and OPL's (One Point Lessons) to document product

specifics and tribal knowledge. This was a long-involved process that took a year.

2. Implement "feeder lines" off of the main glazing process for specific metal cuts. Pull these lines into the main process. This is blasphemy to many Lean professionals but was the right solution here.

3. Implement Mixed Model Sequencing on the SGD line, so it would make multiple products each day. This balanced capacity, made them more flexible, and enable more business for the company.

None of this was quick or easy, but the objective was eventually met.

CHAPTER EIGHT
COMMENTARY ON OTHER INDUSTRIES- HEALTHCARE AND MILITARY

Health Care

Although I have no direct experience in Health Care, and I find the Lean Hospital work not useful, my experience with interviews, personal patient experience, and basically my Lean thinking mind, here are some stories and observations.

1. Health care should be focused on root cause of the dis-ease and the preventative countermeasure to prevent recurrence. It seems to me that instead Health Care focuses on symptoms (non-root) causes and non-preventative cures, called medication.

2. Lack of integration with alternative healing modalities. In Lean, there needs to be a merger of tools, culture, and leadership. Within tools there are many types, and the ability to integrate the tools is key. Health care needs to integrate traditional tools with alternative healing tools. After all, Lean is basically "alternative medicine" for companies, when other things don't work. When I was hospitalized recently, after nine days lying on my back, I was taken for a six-minute walk, and based on the Oxygen uptake reading, would have to wear oxygen tanks for the rest of my life. There was no root cause analysis, including the reduction of oxygen from being completely inert for nine days.

3. Doctors egos need to diminish. A colleague shared a story with me, that I have no reason to doubt. There are thousands of incidents where surgical instruments were left inside patients. A team of surgical nurses suggested a checklist, where instruments brought in had to correlate with the amount of instruments removed from the operating room. Basically, a simple checks and balances system. The doctors completely dismissed the system, saying they couldn't make those kinds of mistakes. 200,000 instruments left inside patients suggest otherwise.

4. By the way, health care professionals are as frustrated, if not more so, that we are. The "system" calls out for change. Lean principles can be helpful. I was talking to a Nurse/Practitioner the other day, and she is terrific. She is very frustrated with the insurance system, which often time does not pay for preventative procedures, but does pay when something goes wrong.

US Air Force- Robbins Air Force Base Georgia

There are two stories, one successful, one not so much, in the US Air Force, who embraced Lean in the early 2000's

This part of the base repaired F15 fighters, C5 Cargo planes and other aircraft and was the first known military facility to introduce Lean. I was part of the project team briefly, with the group of other consultants, and take no credit for the results. I must admit that the methodology, which was quite effective, is against my "Lean Religion", and was based largely on "events". But it took several false starts and 10 years to get there. As a matter of fact, they used many of the Lean methods I eschew, and still were successful, despite Leadership changes and market challenges. Here are the tools they used.

- 6S (Straighten, Sort, Shine, Standardize, Sustain, and Safety)
- Value stream mapping
- Rapid improvement events (i.e., kaizen events)
- Standard work
- Point-of-use (POU) storage
- Cellular manufacturing / one-piece flow
- Strategy alignment and deployment (i.e., policy deployment or hoshin kanri)

And, of course, their heavy use of consultants is also an issue for me. But it's the US military, and with unlimited time and money, perhaps this is a good process. It's just one many of us can't afford.

Sorry for the real or perceived bitterness.

In the interest of fairness, here are some results:

Chemical Point-of-Use Cabinets and Waste Collection

Robins AFB instituted lean, point-of-use (POU) cabinet systems for hazardous materials used on the shop floor to reduce the time and distance that workers travel to retrieve hazardous materials. These chemical POU storage cabinets have initial accumulation points associated with them for collecting hazardous wastes from work cells. Robins AFB designed and implemented these POU systems using lean rapid process improvement events, 6S, and visual controls. In addition, Robins AFB has developed a POU request form that allows ESOH personnel to review proposals for POU cabinets and ensure that the applicable requirements will be met for each chemical included in the cabinets. Installing POU cabinets has reduced travel time, saved 1,500 miles of worker travel, and decreased hazardous materials use and hazardous waste generation by 20 percent on the flight line, even while production was increasing. In one shop, hazardous materials usage and hazardous waste generation decreased by 50 percent.

Applying Lean to Hazardous Waste Management Processes

Robins AFB applied lean techniques—such as Value-Stream Mapping, standard work, and 6S— to its hazardous waste management processes to reduce the lead time for collecting and hauling away hazardous wastes. After examining the non-value added time in its process, Robins AFB instituted a new system for collecting and transporting hazardous wastes; this system eliminated process steps, saved 1,500 hours of time handling wastes, and reduced the frequency that waste drums were handled (decreasing the number of times waste drums were touched by workers by 70 percent). Robins AFB also reorganized its hazardous waste management facility using 6S and visual controls to control inventory and work in process as well as improve flow. This made it easier to monitor the waste management processes and reduced the likelihood of accidents and spills.

Other Lean Projects and Results

Robins AFB has implemented a variety of other lean projects that have had environmental implications, such as the following examples.

- C-5 Maintenance Shop: Lean improvements in the C-5 cargo plane shop reduced "flow days" from 360 to 220 days, improved resource productivity by 30-50 percent, and saved $8 million in the first year alone. These improvements reduced raw material consumption, hazardous chemicals use, and waste associated with the C-5 maintenance processes.
- C-130 Aircraft Paint Shop: Robins AFB used 6S techniques to improve its paint system for the C-130 Hercules airplanes. Through a series of lean events, Robins AFB reduced flow days, increased production, improved worker safety, and reduced volatile organic compound (VOC) emissions, chemical use, and storage space.

So, the question for me, is could these great improvements have been done is a more streamlined, less costly process. That is for you to decide.

The not so great Air Force Story:

Unfortunately, when the Air Force tried to spread to other Air Force Maintenance bases, or area beyond maintenance, it ran into snags and problems. My consulting input was to try a new approach, which was not taken on kindly. The concept of how you turn a 40000-ton ship around, is of course, very slowly. Sadly, this process applies to all US military operations. So, Rapid Deployment is an oxymoron to Lean. Keep in mind that all of these initiatives are "federally funded", which will go without commentary, but many of us do not have the luxury of unlimited time and money. It accentuates the problems of Lean being implemented for results in industries that have non-sufficient time, money or resources to make these changes.

Spiritual Lessons from Doing Lean

Finally, a learning about how my Lean career informed my life, for me in rather profound ways. The story about the Boamah in Kuala Lumpur was one example, that opened my eyes to other ways of doing things. Another happened after a trip to Singapore. I had a 26-hour flight back to my home in Florida and had nothing to read. I stopped in the airport bookstore, and a book almost literally spoke to me, and said, "Read Me". This was odd, as it was a spiritual book, and I didn't have a spiritual bone in my body. Or, so I thought. It was Marianne Williamson's, "Return to Love", and it changed my life. I finished it on the plane ride home, joined a local Course in Miracles group, which was in a Unity church. I started my 30-year experience with Unity, which is, perhaps, another book. It cumulated in me going to ministerial school in 2015 and becoming an ordained minister in 2017. Lean allowed me to travel, and have many different religious and spiritual experiences, a few of which are listed below. Further, Lean opened my mind to new ways of doing things and thinking about things.

Accidently, Lean taught me another important lesson about materialism. I had a nice, lucrative career, and nice townhouse on the beach, a nice car, and lots of nice stuff. Then, I was thrust into a situation where I was on the road for three years to support multinational client sites. And, I mean three years straight…six sites, two weeks a quarter each. So, I sold all my possessions and reduced things to a duffel bag and a laptop computer. Talk about 5S and elimination of waste! From those days forward, I've never longed for things or possessions.

Time in the Far East allowed me many experiences when I wasn't working. I attended a fire walking ceremony, and actually participated and learned how to do it. I witnessed a sword swallowing demonstration. I attended Buddhist meditation retreats, and saw orange clad monks in Thailand, begging for alms in the morning. I was awakened by Islamic prayers at 3:30 a.m. over a loudspeaker in Shah Alam and participated in Deepavali and Ramadan. All these experiences informed my like and career.

Best wishes to all of you brave souls attempting to implement Lean. It is a highly challenging and rewarding journey. Feel free to contact me at any time with questions and comments. To learn more on the Spiritual journey, my next book will be on my 30 years in Spiritual Life. Somehow, they have merged together.

CHAPTER NINE
A SIMPLE, PRACTICAL GUIDE ON HOW TO DO THIS

Let's explore three scenarios: The first one, you are called in to "start Lean" or "Continuous Improvement", with a willing Management team who wants the learn.

The second is a company that has tried Lean, or a derivative, one or more times before, and wants to "restart" due to a variety of reasons.

The third is a company that has been doing this for quite some time and wants to "take it to the next level".

Of course, all of these motives should be questioned. Companies are almost always overly optimistic about their progress with Lean. I really admire the few who say. "We really suck at this and need help". I have experienced all of these scenarios, many times in my career, and offer the following advice.

Scenario 1: Just starting Lean

Assess the current situation with a "Lean set of Eyes". Take three weeks to assess current operations, without judgement, using data collection, interviews with employees and Gemba methods. Have a script for what questions to ask, and what data to collect. Empirically and intuitively determine what key business issues are. This is a three-week process and is nonnegotiable- organizations think they know what the problems are...insist on an "outside set of eyes". Review KPI's to see if they are leading in the right direction. More than likely, they are not.

Then, find "Herbie", the constraint in the process you are working. Inventory is a good guide, as is data on defects, customer complaints and the like. Teach "Problem Solving" to everybody in the process. Set up VCS (Visual Control Systems) in the targeted process. If it is an equipment intensive process, start TPM and gather equipment loss data.

In all cases form teams. They could be TPM teams, Small Group Activities, Quality Circles, or whatever. Make sure they are cross functional and cross level. Train them on Team Dynamics and Star points, as well as Problem Solving.

Spend a lot of time on the floor. It matters what you do out there. Process observation, talking with operators, looking at data. Put your desk on the floor if possible.

Start Leadership training, but don't ask them to do anything yet. Make sure they understand the concepts of Lean, and how their behavior will be asked to change over the course of the process.

This "beginning" will take three to six months. Don't do 5S or run any Kaizen events. Have a trusted "guru" to bounce ideas off of. Find internal resources who can be future leaders/ influencers in the process. (Find Sherry)

Don't mention the word "Lean" if possible. Or Continuous Improvement, or Operational Excellence; just do the work.

After this period, present findings to Senior Management. Do not sugarcoat or pander for more work. Simply lay out the findings. Insist on a Hoshin Session, which is mandatory, to see where the highest impact projects are. Do not move forward without this. Teach the importance of Lean as a Business Strategy Process, rather than a Manufacturing Improvement process. Study, train, and insist on this, and be well trained on how to do Strategic Deployment. If you don't feel capable, get a consultant. This is where the paths diverge somewhat.

If the company is new to Lean or Continuous Improvement, discern if the operation needs "proof of concept", before doing anything significant. Suggest two or three areas that are critical to business success, theoretically "Herbies", and go to work there.

Then, do the off site three day. Move forward with what it says. Develop Sharepoint applications and ways to share information. Move quickly on the momentum created by the offsite event. Form and train teams in how to work the process which for most, will be quite different from what they are used to.

Start Leadership training. If you don't know how to do this, find someone who does. Slowly, practice methods to encourage proper Leadership and behavior. Conduct Cross functional team meetings, or "Kaizens" if you must call them that to drive Strategic Action plans. Take Leaders on Gemba walks and show them how to do them.

Scenario 2: Been here before, didn't work

Find out the 5Why as to the reason for the previous failure. And, as importantly, find out why "Now is different". Did new corporate Leadership come in.? Did business conditions worsen?

Are there new personal who have been there, done that, and are "experienced Lean practitioners"? If so, interview them, and see if you are "on the same page". It's not likely that you are.

Review with Management. Be sure they understand what you are asking for. Ask for approval to proceed. If so, ask if there is agreement on the approach.

Scenario 3: Take it to the next level.

Ask, "what is the next level"? Then proceed with the above steps.

In all cases, do as many things on the "list", and don't do as many of the "don'ts" as possible.

Lean Do's

I was advised by a mentor never to complain about a problem, unless I had a solution to it. So, here goes:

1. KISS, keep it simple, silly
2. "Catch ball" metrics throughout the process.
3. Understand deeply what Lean is and is not about. It is not about elimination of waste, reducing cost, fixing manufacturing issues, or other preconceived notions.
4. Drill problems to root cause and preventative countermeasures. Don't band aid or cover up problems.
5. Do Strategic Planning and Hoshin Deployment to create balanced implementation
6. Do VCS instead of 5S
7. Understand the Spirit of Kaizen, rather than the event approach
8. Monitor the right metrics
9. Focus on equipment losses instead of OEE.
10. Teach Lean leadership and practice it
11. Promote "problems are good" and drive a process to resolve them.
12. Develop a problem-solving process and deploy it.

13. Do only a few strategic objectives, no more than three, and manage them via the Hoshin process.
14. Look for areas outside of Manufacturing to do Lean.
15. Look to replace parts of MRP with replenishment, try PFEP.
16. Look at your Product Costing system, to see it accurately reflects costs.
17. Look at your HR and People systems, to see if they actually support people.
18. Hire, or contract with a Lean Leader who knows what they are doing…they are rarer than you think.

So, 18 tips seem to violate KISS, but many of them are self-apparent. KISS refers to being intuitive and using common sense, and not so reliant on experts and formulas, Have fun, learn from the process and enjoy.

Breaking down the Don'ts and Dos'

1. There are no Standard Recipe's. This is quite like cooking. Personal touches and industry quirks are required to make the perfect dish. Take the perfect recipe and perfect it with your industry and personal touch.
2. 5S has been and perhaps always will be, perceived as a Cleanliness and Housekeeping program. Even worse, monitored and measured by scorecards. This is both professionally and personally insulting. Focus instead on how to identify and solve problems. It is a much better personal and professional approach.
3. Do Hoshin, or some form of Strategic planning. Link Lean projects to key company strategies and

objectives. Choose a small number of Business process to analyze and improve.

4. Drive Kaizen as a daily activity to improve the process, rather than as an "event". Teach daily process observation and commentary.

Lean Don'ts

1. Don't follow a standard implementation recipe. There are principles and practices, but each Lean site is unique and different.

2. Don't start with 5S, or 6S including Safety. 5S had become a housekeeping program, which most floor operators find demeaning and offensive. Do VCS instead.

3. Don't do pilots. Pilots prove nothing. Connect key business strategic needs to Lean implementation. Make initial work critical business important.

4. Don't do 3-5-day Kaizen events. Study the true Spirit of Kaizen, which is daily improvement at the point of the work.

5. Don't pick the wrong problems to work on. This is a very common error. Ask and get consensus on the most important and root cause problems to work on.

6. Don't teach the wrong things; teach problem solving and resolution of problems, not elimination of waste, value stream maps, and 5S.

7. Don't focus on OEE for equipment. Focus on equipment losses instead and have OEE be a result.

8. Don't start without a Leadership commitment. Make sure it is a commitment, with deliverables and

actions, and not "support", the most dangerous word in Leadership.

9. Don't focus only on Manufacturing. Cross functional supply chain things are much more likely to have major business impact.

10. Don't spend a lot of time on Value Stream Mapping. Time is better spent on line analysis of problems and countermeasures.

11. Don't hire consultants who don't know what they are doing. Ask them their process, their recipe and their approach. If it doesn't link with yours, walk away. Don't ever accept that they will teach you how to do lean or help you reduce your costs.

12. Don't make it an objective to reduce cost. See above. Cost reduction is a result, not a strategy.

13. Don't abide reluctant or unwilling leaders, no matter who they are, or how technically proficient. Find exit strategies, internally or externally for these people. You know who they are.

14. Don't make promises to employees you can't possibly keep, e.g. no layoffs. Tell the truth, more quickly, and more honestly. Understand, Lean can do only so much for business cycles.

15. Don't make the work harder for the employees than it already is. A key Lean objective, often forgotten, is to make the work easier for employees. Better tools, better flow, better communication.

16. Don't do Leadership standard work. Get Leadership to the floor for Huddles and Gemba walks.

17. Don't do Six Sigma or train Green Belts. Focus on Lean first instead. There is no value in reducing defects in an unstable process. Plus, Six Sigma, is by its nature, non-participatory.

18. Supermarkets are for groceries, not parts. Don't put WIP parts on the floor and say it's a Lean thing.
19. Don't ignore company culture, it is quite real. Understand what it is and how to deal with it. Study deeply.

Review the lists carefully, review with your team and Senior Management, and make an improvement plan.

Note, I have done all of the above Don'ts, over a long period of time. They are the lessons I have learned.

So, what is the DNA of Lean? What can you replicate throughout your organization through departments, generations, levels and structures? What can DNA teach us about how to implement Lean? First of all, DNA is extraordinarily simple. Only four enzymes, out of thousands possible, combines to make a DNA molecule. So, keep it simple. Then, it's about the RNA, which is how the message is communicated. Make sure the Lean message is consistent with the message being sent in every other way. Conflicts in the message will kill the process. Allow mutations, things specific to your process or culture that need to be allowed. Finally, consider the double helix (tools and culture), without which the process would not work. Combine tools with Leadership and Culture change to allow the process to work best. Blessings on your journey.

CHAPTER TEN
APPENDICES AND CHARTS

Appendix 1: Lean Glossary of Terms:

A-3 Problem Solving Process: Based on a British Paper size, the process tries to identify key elements of a problem, get to root cause, and identify preventative countermeasures. Known for its ability to summarize on one page, and ask, "Do we have the right problem"

Activity Based Costing: A lean finance method that seeks to determine actual product costs, rather than allocations. Seeks to see how volume, mix and price affects costs, with the outcome to make more of the profitable products and make decisions about less profitable ones.

Activity Board: An in line display board that show all current activity about problem solving in a process. Updated and Maintained by Team members.

Agile: A term originally meant for manufacturing flexibility, but now mostly a design and IT term.

Autonomous Maintenance: A TPM concept to allow operators to do simple Maintenance tasks. Defined by the "Transfer Zone", indicating what traditional maintenance tasks could be done by operations. Starts with Initial Inspection.

Backflush: A method to transact all items on a Bill of Material upon product completion, rather than transactions for each part. A way to reduce transaction volume and errors.

Bill of Materials. In Lean, the "flatter the better", which means eliminating sub-assemblies as discrete transacted units, and moving toward a "pile of parts mentality"

CANDO: A derivative of 5S. An acronym standing for Clean, Arrange, Neatness, Discipline and Order. Learned from Yamaha Motorcycle.

CEDAC: Cause and Effect diagram with the addition of Cards. A nine-step problem solving process, used in the Equipment improvement process. It is known for its visual nature.

Continuous Improvement: A generic term describing a variety of improvement initiatives within a company suggesting a lack of direction or focus on what the strategy actually is.

Containment: When a problem's root cause is identified, and not solved, but something is done to deal with the problem in the meantime.

Corrective Action: An action to permanently resolve a problem identified in a process.

Demand Flow Technology: The basic JIT methodology with the addition of Pull and Kanban systems in support.

Design for Assembly: A method to get into the Design process to make sure products are assemblable rather than just a conceptual design.

Design for Manufacturability: Extends the above concept to supplier parts (go for standardization) and simple ways to put parts together, remembering the concept of making the work easier for operators.

EFFlow: A system to turn off MRP and rely on pull to rely on shop operations.

Equipment Improvement process: A 13-week process to reduce equipment losses and improve Overall Equipment Effectiveness.

Equipment Losses: Any state of equipment that is not running good product at optimal speed.

Five S: A housekeeping program, disguised as an improvement methodology. Often called 6S, when mistakenly combined with safety.

FMEA: Failure modes and Effects Analysis. A ranking system to evaluate which are the most serious problems to work on. Use an RPI (Rank Priority Index) to rank issues. A more elaborate version of the Impact Control Matrix.

Gemba Walks: Going to the spot, and engaging employees on what their problems are, and how you can help.

Hejunka: A system a line balancing and leveling.

Huddles: A five to ten-minute walk through at the beginning of the day, to "call the play" on what is important for the day.

Initial Clean and Inspection: A TPM term aiming to operators to identify all defects and problems in their work, and also be aware of problems as they occur.

JIT: Just in Time. The original term to describe the Toyota Production System. Replaces "Just in Case" manufacturing common in manufacturing and office.

Kanban: An intermediate WIP storage are to encourage pull, and to recognize process cycle time differentials. A key ingredient of Demand Pull. A method to directly recognize downstream demand, so that no excess is produced. The original term for deploying Lean to the US.

Lean Manufacturing: A term suggesting that Lean applies to Manufacturing, exclusively, first, or in a vacuum. A dangerous approach.

Lean Enterprise: A broader approach that suggests that Lean principles apply to all areas of the business, Supply chain and Support functions, and sees the interconnectedness of the functions.

Lean Six Sigma: An idea that suggests the merger of two seemingly divergent technologies; one to make processes stable and reliable, and the other to reduce variation within the process.

Mixed Model Sequencing: The idea of running multiple models, with common process characteristics, down a single line, and effectively responding to the downstream pull process.

Materials Requirements Planning: Also called ERP. A computer system popularized by Oliver Wight and others in the 1960's and 70s, in an attempt to forecast and complete material and production needs.

Non-Value-added Activity: Anything the customer doesn't pay for, or does not transform form, fit or function.

Overall Equipment Effectiveness: Actual production divided by theoretical production.

Policy for Every Part, (PFEP): A method for determining which approach is best for each part, Repetitive, Min/Max, MRP controlled or other.

Planned Maintenance: A TPM pillar for developing the most effective Maintenance Strategies for an Operation

Repetitive Manufacturing: another term for JIT in the 80's and 90's, Repetitive manufacturing (REM) is the production of goods in rapid succession. Goods that are created through repetitive manufacturing follow the same production sequences.

Six Sigma- An improvement process attempting to reduce variation, which has been distorted by America to train Green and Black belts to do Lean projects. A non-participatory, engineering driven process to deduce variation. Literally, a process that has less than 3.4 defects per million opportunities. Introduced by Motorola in the early 1990's. Uses the DMAIC process to drive defects down.

Theory of Constraints: A method to define the process constraint. Once identified, resources should be directed to it, in order to eliminate it. Initiated by Eli Goldratt, an Israeli physicist.

Value Added: Something the customer pays for. Something that involves, form, fit or function of the product. Typically, about 15-20% of product activity.

Value Stream Mapping: A process to identify the process, inventory, and problem points in a process

Appendix 2 Charts.

Lower the water, uncover the rocks

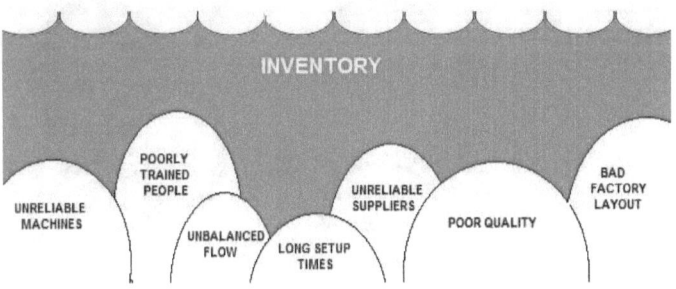

Single Cause, Multiple Cause and Complex Combinational
Cause Problems

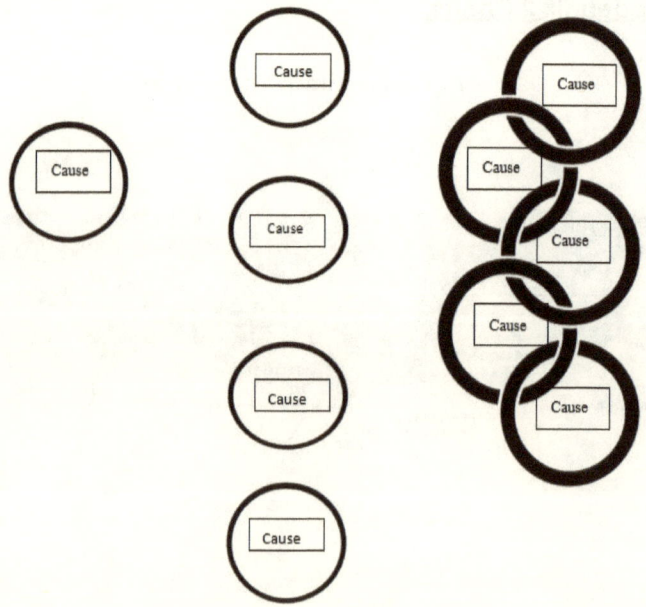

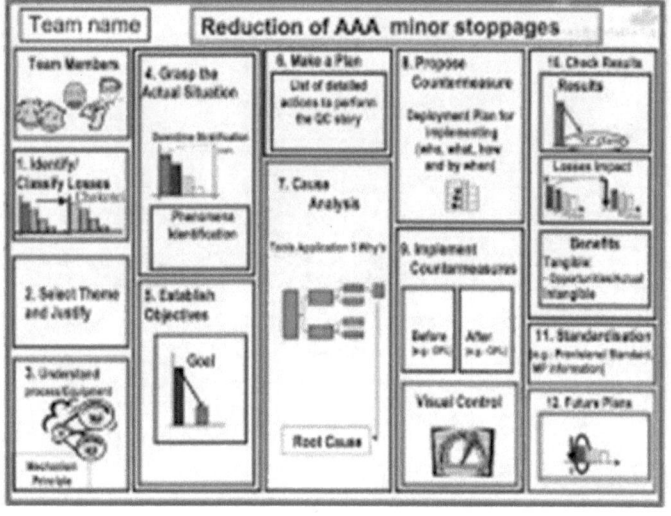

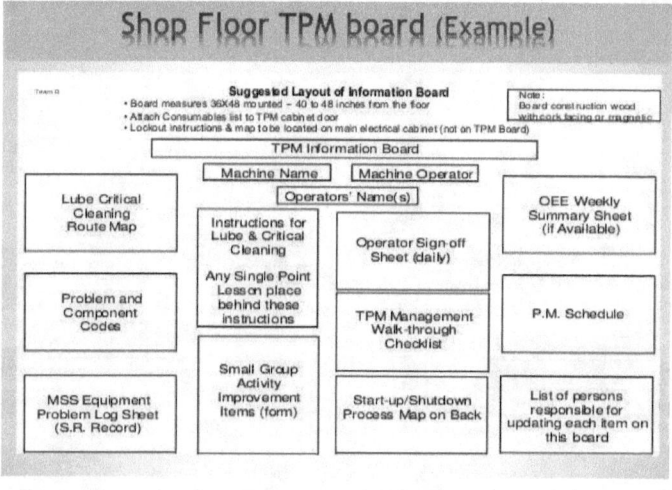

Shop Floor TPM board (Example)

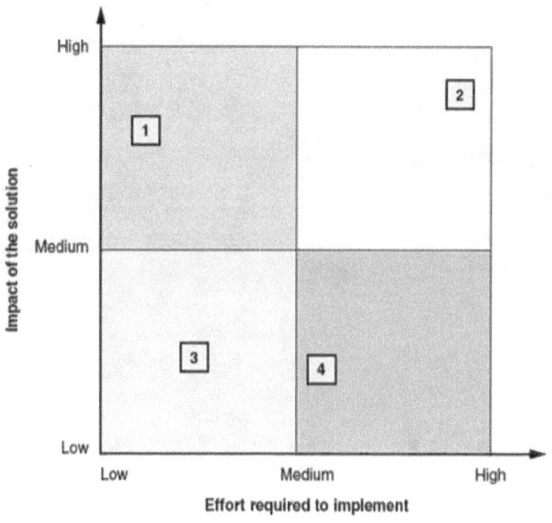

A3

Title   **Name(s)**   **Date**

Background:

Why you are talking about it.

What is the business reason for choosing this issue?

Current Conditions:

Where things stand today.
- What's the problem with that, with where we stand?
- What is the actual symptom that the business feels that requires action?

Show visually – pareto charts, graphs, drawings, maps, etc.

Target(s)/Goal(s)

The specific outcome required for the business.
- What is the specific change you want to accomplish now.?
- How will you measure success?

Analysis

The root cause(s) of the problem.
- Why are we experiencing the symptom?
- What constraints prevent us from the goal?
Choose the simplest problem-solving tool for this issue:
- 5 Whys
- Fishbone
- QC Tools
- OC Tools

Proposed Countermeasure(s):

Your proposal to reach the future state, the target condition.
- What alternatives could be considered?
- How will you choose among the options? What decision criteria?

How your recommended countermeasures will impact the root cause to
change the current situation and achieve the target.

Implementation Plan:

A chart or table that shows actions/outcomes, timeline and responsibilities.

May include details on the specific means of implementation.
- Who will do what, when and how?

Indicators of performance, of progress.
- How will we know if the actions have the impact needed?
- What are the critical few, visual, most natural measures?

Follow Up:

Remaining issues that can be anticipated.
- Any failure modes to watch out for? Any unintended consequences?

Ensure ongoing P-D-C-A.

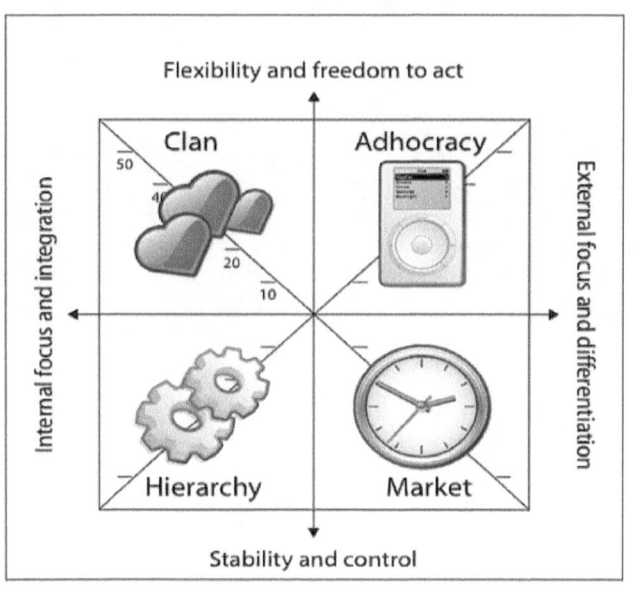

Flexibility and freedom to act

Clan

Adhocracy

Internal focus and integration

External focus and differentiation

Hierarchy

Market

Stability and control

KANBAN BOARD

Kanban Card

Part Number		QTY
	Due Date	
		To
From		
	Number: (e.g. 1 of 3)	

www.ingramcontent.com/pod-product-compliance
Lightning Source LLC
Chambersburg PA
CBHW030741180526
45163CB00003B/875